THIS BOOK IS GAY

JUNO DAWSON

ILLUSTRATIONS BY SPIKE GERRELL

HOT
KEY

This book is dedicated to anyone
who has ever wondered.

First published in Great Britain in 2014 by HOT KEY BOOKS
80–81 Wimpole St, London W1G 9RE
www.hotkeybooks.com

A CIP catalogue record for this book is available from the British Library.

ISBN: 978-1-4714-0395-8
also available as an ebook

6

Printed and bound by Clays Ltd, St Ives Plc

Hot Key Books is an imprint of Bonnier Publishing Fiction,
a Bonnier Publishing company
www.bonnierpublishingfiction.co.uk
www.bonnierpublishing.co.uk

CONTENTS

Author's note:

This Book Is Gay is a collection of facts, my ideas and my stories but also the testimonies of more than three hundred amazing LGBT* people who shared their stories. In July 2013, I conducted an international survey from which many of the quotes are taken, and also carried out more in-depth interviews with some selected participants.

As not all of the participants are 'out' or open about their sexuality, or may have sensitive careers, some names have been changed.

Throughout *This Book Is Gay*, I've used LGBT* to represent the full and infinite spectrum of sexual and gender identities. It's certainly not my intention for anyone to feel excluded by that initialism; I just needed a shorthand or the book would have been a LOT longer!

A huge thank you to everyone who took part. I'm so proud of what we've achieved with this book.

Juno Dawson

CHAPTER 1:

WELCOME TO THE MEMBERS CLUB

Lesson One

- Sometimes men fancy men.

- Sometimes women fancy women.

- Sometimes women fancy men and women.

- Sometimes men fancy women and men.

- Sometimes people don't fancy anyone.

- Sometimes a man might want to be a woman.

- Sometimes a woman might want to be a man.

Got that? It really is that simple.

I could end the lesson, there, but I don't think a few pages would make a very good book, so I *suppose* I should go into a bit more depth . . .

WELCOME TO THE MEMBERS CLUB

There's a long-running joke that, on 'coming out', a young lesbian, gay guy, bisexual or trans person should receive a membership card and instruction manual.

THIS IS THAT INSTRUCTION MANUAL.

You're welcome. But this is a manual for everyone – no matter your gender or sexual preference.

School probably hasn't taught you very much about what it's like to be lesbian, gay, bisexual, trans or questioning. You might have heard about famous gay people or seen same-sex couples on TV. You almost certainly know an LGBT* person, even if you aren't aware of it. Like an 'alien invasion', we are already amongst you. We serve you in the post office; we teach you maths; we fry your fish and chips.

So why don't we teach you about same-sex couples when we teach sex ed? Or that a lot of people choose to change their gender identity from the one they were assigned at birth. Well, I was a PSHCE (Personal, Social, Health and Citizenship) teacher for a long time, and I always taught my students about these things, but not all schools do, and not all teachers know how – there's NO training for this, I'm afraid.

I surveyed a group of more than three hundred young people in 2012, and ninety-five per cent of them said their school taught them NOTHING about gay sex as a part of sex education. Sex between men and women was routinely presented as 'the norm'.

This lack of education means that loads of young people – gay, straight or bi; trans or cis – have oodles of questions about what it's like to be LGBT*. This book has some of the answers. Whether you think you might be LGBT* or you think you're straight but have questions or you're anywhere in between, this book is for you.

Your sexuality or gender is very much an individual thing, but what if there were a whole bunch of people who'd been through it all before to mentor you through this funny old patch?

The awareness that your sexual or gender identity isn't quite the NORM can be a confusing, exciting, exhilarating, concerning and, frankly, baffling time. Long before you 'come out' and tell people about your identity, it's just you and your brain trying to figure it out, so it can also be a lonely time, often accompanied by whiny music and too much eyeliner.

My experience as a gay white man and, more recently, as a trans white woman is not representative of every gay man, let alone the thousands of gay women, bisexual men and women, and trans people who may be reading this book. Therefore, before writing this book, I searched far and wide for dozens of other LGBT* people to share their experiences with you. Individually, we can never know it all, but together we're quite wise, like that baboon in *The Lion King*.

I haven't edited or changed the testimonies of the LGBT* people in this book, so you might not identify with, or agree with, everything they have to say, AND THAT'S FINE. We have to be able to talk about sexuality and identity in a non-hysterical way. Sexuality and gender are individual experiences; people are entitled to opinions and, vitally, we need to be able to make mistakes. I understand identity is an issue that some people feel very strongly about. This is also a good thing – activism is what got us this far – but if people aren't allowed to say what's really on their mind for fear of upsetting people, we'll end up never saying anything at all.

In short, we have to be able to laugh at ourselves, whatever our identity, or we're in for a long-haul life. So, yeah, *This Book Is Gay* isn't entirely serious all the way through (although we do deal with some MEGA-SADFACE topics).

This is something different to the loads of dreary textbooks about gender and sexuality politics that are already out there. This book is serious, but it's also fun and funny.

The whole point of coming out is that we have the FREEDOM to be who we are. When did that stop being FUN?

If you're new to the club, you're lucky because being L or G or B or T or * is SUPER FUN. You're FREE now and don't have to HIDE.

Whatever you identify as by the end of this book, you'll see that, far from being alone, you're joining a vast collective of cool, happy, inspirational people, each with a story to tell.

It's the hippest members' club in town, and you get straight past the velvet rope and into the VIP lounge.

You're not isolated; you're part of something bigger now. Something great.

OH, HI, SEXTHOUGHTS

Let's start at the very beginning (a very good place to start). I guess you're reading this book for one of several reasons. It may be because you already identify as LGBT* (and, let's face it, we love nothing more than talking about it). Maybe you're nosy to see what we get up to between the sheets. It could be you are making fun of it because it has the word 'gay' in the title (shame on you). But maybe, just maybe, you picked up this book because you're WONDERING.

It all starts with wondering.

Wondering what it might be like to kiss that boy, or what that girl's breasts look like. What life would be like if you were a girl, not a guy. It's all about wondering.

WONDERING IS PERFECTLY NATURAL, BUT NEVER ENCOURAGED.

One day I was in the park sunbathing. On the next picnic blanket over, a mother was talking to her infant son about the things he could do when he was older. The conversation went something like this:

Boy: Drive a car!

Mum: Yes!

Boy: Go to work like Daddy!

Mum: Yes!

Boy: Kissing!

Mum: Yes! Girls . . . you'll kiss girls.

After I had snatched the child away and left him with social services (OK, I didn't do that, but I probably should have done something other than tut really loudly), I was sad at how we still DEFAULT to heterosexual in the twenty-first century.

The assumption goes that all babies are born both straight and locked into their birth gender unless something goes awry. This is NOT the case.

- In the UK, a 2010 study showed that five per cent of people did not identify as heterosexual. So about one in twenty people is likely to be 'not-straight'.

- There are an estimated nine million LGBT* people in the US as of 2011.

- A 2009 study estimates there are over ten thousand transgender people living in the UK.

And yet we're all automatically born 'straight' and 'cis' (the gender we're assigned at birth).

Let's do sexuality first. You are told you're straight and assume you're straight for almost all of your childhood, despite quite compelling feelings to the contrary. You believe yourself to be straight (because isn't everyone?) until sexual desire kicks in (assuming it does). I like to call this desire SEXTHOUGHTS.

Because most of us spend our childhood identifying as straight, even though we may or may not actually feel straight, we don't always identify these sexthoughts. But it seems highly likely that from a very young age we, as LGB* people, were attracted to members of the same sex, be it people we know or shiny TV people. (Well, they are pretty fit, right?)

I wanted to know at what stage LGBT* people first had questioning thoughts regarding their sexuality OR gender. So I surveyed hundreds of them.

See figure 1. (Who said statistics had to be boring? Look how pretty that pie chart is!)

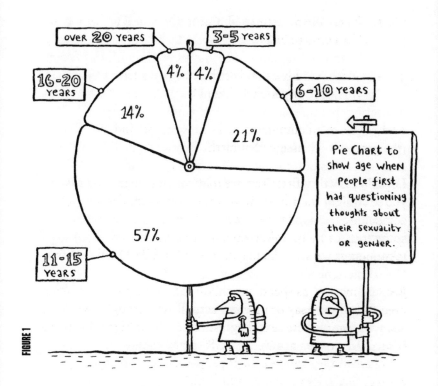

As you can see, a quarter of the sample were having same-sex sexthoughts and/or thoughts regarding their gender before puberty, with over half at puberty.

This makes sense, because puberty is the time at which great changes occur. One big change is the hormonal shift that drives us towards sexual relationships. It is at this point that many of us realise the cheeky little thoughts we're having late at night might be about people with the same bits as us. ESCÁNDALO.

For me it was Dean Cain. Dean Cain, as if you don't know, is the very handsome actor who played Clark Kent in *Lois and Clark: The New Adventures of Superman*. Up until Cain came into my life, I had been convinced I was going to marry a girl in my class called Kelly (whose name I have changed for her protection) because she was kind, friendly and blonde.

However, what I felt for Dean Cain (whose name I did *not* change for this book – I mean, I think IT'S TIME HE KNEW OF MY LOVE) was VERY different to what I felt for Kelly.

My interest in spandex-clad arms was far more pressing than being *fond* of Kelly, and when Clark got together with Lois, I felt the most intense jealousy of my life. (I TOTALLY get how One Directioners feel on Twitter.)

Later, after a massive crush on a male teacher, I had to acknowledge that these feelings went beyond mere appreciation of the male form and were, in fact, sexthoughts.

OH SHITE!

When first faced with same-sex sexthoughts or sexthoughts about your gender, your first reaction may well be the above. After all, society, films, television, newspapers and books have told you your whole life that

STRAIGHT = NORMAL

NOT STRAIGHT = NOT NORMAL.

You have suddenly identified a sexthought that is different. And most people don't like different so, therefore, you're slapped with the NOT NORMAL label.

DON'T PANIC.

Just because LGBT* people are in a minority doesn't mean they are not NORMAL. People with blue eyes are in the minority too, but we don't think of them as abnormal, do we? We don't look at Jake Gyllenhaal and say, LOOK AT THAT MASSIVE BLUE-EYED FREAK! No, we only look at him and weep that we cannot have him. Anyway, who gets to decide what's 'normal' and what isn't? What a horrid, excluding word that is.

You may have grown up not only in the absence of gay or trans role models, but also encountering actual homophobia or transphobia. These things can be hugely worrying – especially at a time when you rely on familial support. You may also be one of the thousands of people born with same-sex sexthoughts in a country where it is illegal to have sexual activity with same-sex partners. (Some people believe same-sex activity is against their religion. More on that in chapter 6.)

You probably have questions. I had LOADS of questions. I'd heard RUMOURS about what two men did together. You may have misunderstood things – my early concept of lesbian sex was way off. (I basically thought it was like sanding the boobs off two Barbie dolls by rubbing them together.) You may have seen odd bits on TV and now don't know what to think. It seems highly likely that any sex ed you had at school taught you only how men and women make babies together and didn't mention transgender people at all.

WHY ARE THERE TRANS PEOPLE IN THIS BOOK?

You are right to ask this. 'Lesbian', 'gay', 'bisexual' and the other orientations we talk about in this book are about sexuality. Being transgender has nothing to do with who you want to do sexytime with – it's about gender.

Trans people and non-straight people are subject to a lot of the same discrimination, misunderstanding and mistreatment, because many people think of us as all being part of the same group. In a way, we are – and that's why many people use 'LGBT' as shorthand for our whole community. That initialism is inclusive of 'trans', so this manual should be too.

What's more, if we wanted to, we all could spend our lives hiding. Whether I liked it or not, I fancied blokes, but I could have SO EASILY lied and pretended to like girls. I could have married a girl like Kelly and been utterly miserable, but instead I accepted an identity and did something about it. So do all proud lesbians, gay men, bi, curious and queer people. **And so do transgender people**. As with sexual diversity, trans people **could** say, 'This is too scary,' and spend life stuck with the wrong gender identity.

So whether it's LGB* or T, we're all seeking membership to this awesome club that exists outside the majority. And that's why we're all in this (book) together.

ThinGS No ONE saYS EVER

When did you realise you were straight?

Does your mum know you're straight?

When you have straight sex, is one of you the woman?

I have a straight friend – would you like me to set you up on a date?

It was so much fun – we went dancing at a straight club!

I went to the cutest straight wedding at the weekend.

Do you think straight people should be allowed to have kids?

I don't mind straight people kissing, but I wish they wouldn't rub our faces in it.*

*There is a special place in Hades for ALL people – gay, straight or otherwise – who kiss with visible tongue / audible slurping in public places.

CHAPTER 2:

THE NAME GAME

So, you may have SEXTHOUGHTS about people of the same gender as you, OR you may have questions regarding your own gender. Loads of people – even people who end up identifying as straight and cis – have these thoughts and questions. I think it's far odder to have NEVER thought about it. I'm a gay man, but I've considered having sexyfuntime with women plenty of times. Funnily enough, it's yet to 'turn me'.

This is all fine. The fact that you've identified your sexthoughts is probably the hardest part, so reward yourself with a delicious bun or cake.

BUT now we get to the bit where you actually have to make a choice.

> 1. You can choose to do nothing. You can sit on these feelings and hope they go away.

> 2. You can acknowledge them and act on them – do the sex you wanna do or wear the clothes you wanna wear – but choose not to define yourself.

> 3. You can act on them AND adopt an identity to define yourself. This is the bit where you'd get the membership card and become part of a community.

Wowsers, this whole gay thing is a lot more complicated than *Glee* led us to believe.

People with same-sex sexthoughts or uncertainty about their gender sometimes stop at option one, but I think these people are probably very sad and angry. (I also think a lot of bonkers homophobes are lingering perilously close to option one, and this is what makes them so hateful. Freud called it 'transference'. This basically means that you hate in others what you hate about yourself.)

More people choose option two – you can **totally** have sex with people who are the same gender as you and not be 'gay' or 'lesbian' or 'bi'. This is why a lot of forms (especially medical ones) you fill in may refer to 'men who have sex with men', etc.

You have very little choice about your sexual preference or gender, but you can decide whether to make it a lifestyle. This is option three: you get to be out and proud and open about your relationships or gender. Living with stress and secrets is both stressful and secretive.

It's human nature to label things, and if you're having some confusing thoughts, giving a name to the situation may make you feel better because you can be part of something – a bigger support network – the International Haus of Gay, if you will. I present the identity machine. Start at the top and see where it takes you!

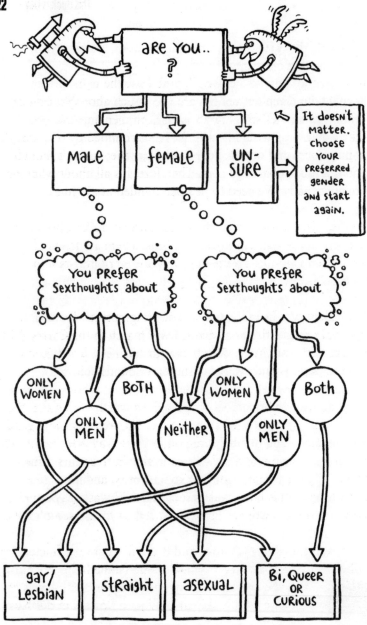

SEX PIGEONS

Before we go any further, you'll note I use the word prefer.
Sexuality and gender identity are very much about preference.
I think we all CONSIDER sex with both men and women.
Like I said, why wouldn't we? We're surrounded by sexy images
in magazines and on TV. People who say they haven't thought
about it are probably fibbers. Therefore, it's all about what we
prefer sexually. We need to be open minded at all times.

It's also worth noting that there are stacks of folks who don't
like any of the above sexuality options. There are loads of
pigeonholes to stuff people into, but not everyone fits into
them so easily.

Your identity is as individual as your fingerprints. Frankly, if
you want to identify as a carrot, I will march in the Carrot Pride
parade with you. Your identity is your business. It's all gravy.
In fact, pigeons and carrots with gravy sounds delish.

Now that we've been label shopping, it's worth noting that the
one you bought has a return policy. Sexual preference and gender
are **fluid**, meaning just because you feel one way now, it doesn't
necessarily mean you'll feel the same way in five years' time.
Plenty of people change their sexual identity, and that's fine.
In fact, when this book was first published I was a gay man.
Now I'm a trans woman! That's just the way it goes, ain't it.

So if everything's changeable, and if we all exist on a fluctuating,
wibbly-wobbly spectrum of sexual desire (something very hard
to define at the best of times), why do we bother with labels at
all? Why don't we all just skip around with flowers in our hair

making out with the people we fancy, regardless of their gender? Well, probably because that's quite hard to describe. At the end of the day, it's easier to have a single word to use to define yourself when talking to other people. People will ask you how you identify and, although it's tempting to launch into a tirade about the tyranny of labels, it's far simpler to say, 'Oh, I'm bi,' and let that be it. Still, even that doesn't mean you HAVE to adopt a label; plenty of people don't.

With this in mind let's take a look at the most common labels on offer at the Identity Shop.

L IS FOR LESBIAN

The word lesbian is derived from the name of the island of Lesbos, where a Greek poet called Sappho ran her own sixth-century BC version of *The L Word*. She gathered a whole gang of girls in the sunshine and wrote poems about how hot they were. Fast forward twenty-five hundred years, to around the turn of the twentieth century, and women were seeking a name for a growing subculture that was gaining visibility and status. Until this point, historically, gay women were almost considered a myth – probably a sign of how little women were regarded

MARS BAR/SNICKERS CONTINUUM

100%
FANCY
WOMEN

or thought of as sexual creatures outside of marriage.

But now, gay women, inspired by Sappho's island of lusty ladies, coined the name 'lesbian', which before then had been used to describe anything 'of Lesbos'.

Today the word more or less means 'a woman who has sex with women'. Some such women don't like the word 'lesbian' and prefer 'gay woman'.

'I prefer "gay" to "lesbian" - I think it's something about the noun vs. adjective thing, i.e. "lesbian" sounds a bit more central and defining, whereas "gay" is just one of a number of adjectives that could be used to describe a person.'

J, 28, Brighton.

Now. You may have heard some people calling lesbians 'dykes'. This is a touchy subject because it originated as an insulting term. **Unless you identify as lesbian yourself, you should never use the word 'dyke' at all.** The word is pejorative unless it's being reclaimed as slang by gay women themselves.

100% FANCY MEN

G IS FOR GAY

The word 'gay' started life meaning joyful, carefree, bright and showy, from the French term 'gaiety', which is still used. However, by the seventeenth century, the word had evolved: a 'gay woman' was a prostitute, a 'gay man' was promiscuous, and a 'gay house' was a brothel. Nice.

So, by the mid-twentieth century, gay still meant 'carefree' – as opposed to those who were 'straight' or a little square – and started to take on its homosexual connotations. Given that at the time 'homosexual' was a clinical diagnosis, it's no wonder that a term meaning 'bright and showy' ironically became shorthand for men who wished to exist in a secret subculture.

By the 1990s, it was decided that 'gay' was the preferred and politically correct way to refer to men who have sex with men (and, of course, also women who have sex with women).

Sadly, at about the same time, the word 'gay' was also twisted to mean something that was weak, crap or rubbish. I don't care what anyone says, this usage stems from homophobia, so don't do it. YES, I KNOW IT'S IN THE TITLE, BUT THAT'S BECAUSE I'M MAKING A POINT – EVERYTHING IN THIS BOOK IS ABOUT ACTUALLY BEING GAY (or lesbian or bi or trans or *, but that wouldn't have been nearly as attention grabbing, would it?).

B IS FOR BISEXUAL

This is nothing new. The people of ancient Greece and Rome were generally pansexual (people who are sexually attracted to people regardless of their gender or sexuality), and no one batted an eyelid. Sadly for us, we like things to be binary: black/white, good/bad, male/female. And this isn't great for anyone.

Broadly speaking, a bisexual is someone who likes to have sex with both men and women. There are a plethora of misunderstandings about bisexuality, the most prevalent being the 'bi now, gay later' theory that all gay men and lesbians have a brief period in Bi-Town before catching the last train to Gayville. While this is the case for some actual gay men and women, there are plenty of people who have no intention of travelling all the way to the end of the line. AND THAT'S FINE.

The idea that bisexual people 'are kidding themselves' or that they are 'being selfish' and/or 'greedy' is hurtful. Why is it so hard to accept that someone might be attracted to both sexes? If someone is willing to identify as bi, then surely they'd be just as happy to wear a 'gay' label. What would be the point in lying? Why do we so badly need people to be gay or straight? Bisexual people might be misunderstood, but they have the right to be PROUD of their identity and sexual preference.

'I identify as lesbian, because I don't like to admit I'm bisexual.'

Blaz, 34, Bristol.

'I identify as bisexual, though I rather like to describe it as "People are beautiful, people are hot, people are attractive, and if I fall in love, I fall in love."'

Mickey, 18, Michigan, USA.

'I tell people I'm bi because it's easier to understand, but I think I'm pan - I'm concerned with personality not genitals.'

Anon, 24, Brighton.

'[I say I'm] bisexual when asked. Varies depending on the day, who I've been around, what I've been reading and so on. A description I found on Tumblr that fits perfectly goes along the lines of "If you think of sexuality in terms of music, where the low notes represent being attracted to boys and high notes represent being attracted to girls, I am a Slayer guitar solo."'

Nina, 16, UK.

Q IS FOR QUEER

'Queer' originally meant someone or something a little unusual or out of the ordinary. In the late twentieth century, it became a derogatory term or abuse word aimed at homosexuals.

However, more recently, following the AIDS pandemic, the word was reclaimed (at first by the group Queer Nation) as a catch-all phrase to represent the full spectrum of sexuality and gender but later as more of a criticism of identity than an identity itself. Basically a label for people – gay or straight – who were sick of labels!

Nonetheless, it is now used as an identity. In the broadest possible terms, as there are a number of groups under the 'queer' umbrella, being queer means not having to define your sexual identity or gender with just one label.

In a world in which your sexuality and gender are open to change, it does sometimes seem silly to use labels. Even classing yourself as bisexual adds to the idea that there are only three choices, which clearly isn't the case – nor should it be an automatic term for someone who is neither gay nor straight.

Queer theory is a fascinating and expanding subject, and there are many, many books and theses written on it.

'Defining yourself with a deliberately slippery word might seem like a contradiction in terms. For me, that was the point. I feel that 'straight', 'gay' and 'bi' don't adequately cover or include the way I feel.

For one thing, those terms suggest a rigid and inflexible take on gender. For people who see sex and gender in any way other than binaries, the options of "one, the other or both" simply don't fit.

In addition to that, I find that gender/sex is a
relatively small part of sexual attraction for
me. It seems odd to define my sexual identity by a small
facet of it. While some people - some LGBT people or
people into kink, for example - choose to solve this
problem with more specific identities, I'd rather not try
and sum it up in that way.

For me, identifying as queer is a way of placing myself
outside straight, mainstream sexuality without having
to identify with other ideas I can't relate to.'

Kerry, Brighton.

C IS FOR CURIOUS

Curious, or questioning, as is often now used, means just that –
someone who is in the process of asking the big questions. I think
all young people should spend time thinking about desire. I think
everyone would be a lot happier if they took a few weeks to dwell
on what does it for them. It'd resolve a lot of tension and grief, I
expect. A whole lot of people 'experiment' – they give it a little go
to see if they like it. Some do, and do it again, and some rule it
out, happy in the knowledge that they're not missing out.

Like anything in life, sometimes you don't know until you try. I
wouldn't eat prawns until I was eighteen – the mere idea of them
freaked me out. But then I tried them and it turns out they're
DELISH. Don't worry, I've more than made up for it since.

(I stress, in this instance, that 'prawns' is not a euphemism for anything.)

A IS FOR ASEXUAL

There are two ways of looking at asexuality. The first is as a lack of, or little interest in, sex (with anyone). The second is as a refusal to define your sexual orientation or uncertainty about your sexual orientation – a more modern use of the term. Asexuality is not celibacy (abstaining from sex). Asexual people MAY have sex – to have kids, to try it out or to experiment – but asexual people will characteristically have little desire for either men or women, so if you go back to our flow chart, they would typically lose interest after the first question.

Asexual people will often have romantic feelings towards people, and they may well have boyfriends and girlfriends and do all the lovey-dovey, holding hands and hugging parts, just without the willies and mimsies.

This is – you guessed it – FINE. Some people just aren't that sexual and, like all identities, this one might change over time. I have found that a growing number of teenagers identify as asexual while figuring out their identity.

T IS FOR TRANSGENDER

Right at the very outset of this discussion, let's not get it twisted.

Here we go:

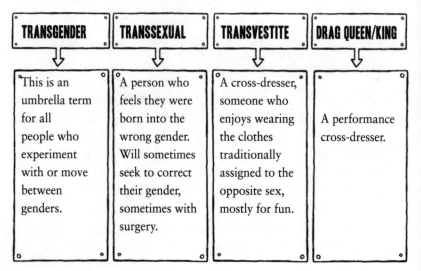

TRANSGENDER	TRANSSEXUAL	TRANSVESTITE	DRAG QUEEN/KING
This is an umbrella term for all people who experiment with or move between genders.	A person who feels they were born into the wrong gender. Will sometimes seek to correct their gender, sometimes with surgery.	A cross-dresser, someone who enjoys wearing the clothes traditionally assigned to the opposite sex, mostly for fun.	A performance cross-dresser.

Now this is really tough, and you'd be forgiven for making mistakes when 'trans' is so often used as shorthand. When it is, it almost certainly means transgender or transsexual. You may also hear **genderqueer**, which, like queer theory regarding sexuality, is more of a refusal to be pigeonholed than an identity in itself.

There are broader issues regarding gender identity, in that we are still very much stuck in a binary culture which says some things are for boys (slugs and snails and puppy-dogs' tails) and some things are for girls (sugar and spice and all things nice – P.S. who wrote this ANTI-FEMINIST HATE ANTHEM? To think we tell it to children in NURSERY).

Advertisers would like us to believe that being female somehow feels different to being male, but we will never really know. Culture tells our parents how to dress us as kids, and it becomes ingrained. It sometimes seems bonkers to me to think that a dude would have to be 'trans' to put on a skirt or some heels. Who bloody says that they are 'female attire'? Sadly, as most of the world is blind to how small-minded this is, that's the way the cookie crumbles. For now.

As we said in the last chapter, although the studies of gender and sexuality are closely linked, they are largely unrelated: a person will choose separate identities for both. For instance, I used to identify as a gay man. Now, I suppose I'm a straight trans woman. You see?

Let's quickly discuss the term 'tranny'. You may have heard this word being bandied about at school or perhaps even on a show like *RuPaul's Drag Race*. Much like 'dyke', unless you are trans, you really shouldn't use it. EVER. This is because a lot of trans people find it offensive, so why would you want to go around upsetting people? Are you a sociopath? No, so don't do it.

RORY'S STORY

Rory from Brighton identifies as a trans man. He had surgery and took hormones to change gender several years ago. Here is his story:

I always liked to dress up and be the boy. At primary school, everyone knew me as 'the girl that wanted to be a boy'. The other kids used to tease me about it in the playground, and it would make me cry, but I didn't know why I was upset by it. Maybe it was the singling out? So I'd get taken aside by my teacher. I couldn't understand what the big deal was; who wouldn't want to be a boy?

As an adult, I found a way of being a boy that was acceptable and adored. I was Rory Raven, drag king extraordinaire! For years I had been dressing up in private, wearing very masculine clothes - shirts with a tie, suits, braces, trilby hat. But I felt I had to hide, that there was something wrong with it. I'd even have to get changed back into my normal clothes just to use the bathroom in my own home, just in case my flatmates saw me. But as a drag king I would be on

stage wearing the clothes publicly that I felt
comfortable wearing. At the end of the performances,
I'd watch my fellow drag kings remove their drag
and change into their regular clothes. They'd scrub
off the fake facial hair and five o'clock shadow
and replace it instead with make-up. Lipstick and
eyeshadow: feminine and understated. I wanted to
stay in my drag and felt at a loss when the evening
was over.

For my twenty-fourth birthday I was given a binder.
A binder is a tight-fitting vest which is worn
underneath clothes that makes the wearer look
flat- chested and, therefore, male. It was tight
and uncomfortable, and wearing it wasn't pleasant.
Getting into it wasn't easy. Getting out was even
harder. I thought I was going to accidentally
suffocate myself trying to take the thing off for
the first time. But wearing it gave me such liberation.
I felt like I was being seen for the first time.
So I kept wearing it, even when I wasn't performing.

Soon enough, I began to wonder: what's the
difference between Rory onstage and Rory in
real life? My friends were already calling
me Rory as a nickname, and some of them were
even referring to me with male pronouns.

I decided to take off the fake beard and just
start living full-time as Rory (only without the
ornithological surname). Work was really supportive.
I know I was lucky in this regard, as I worked for a
trans charity at the time. They didn't bat an eyelid.

My name change was the most important part of my transition. Choosing my name was a profound and powerful decision. It would be a mixture of who I was and who I wanted to be. The timing of my legal change was important too. It was a few days before my twenty-fifth birthday, which for me is the start of my new year, and coincidently was the beginning of the new year for several religions and cultures worldwide.

Life has paradoxically got both better and a lot harder since transition. Coming out to everyone is an ongoing process. Some friends could see it coming, so were unfazed; others took a bit longer and, sadly, I have lost contact with some people altogether. My adopted queer family have embraced me, and that has given me a lot of strength. Transition has opened doors I didn't know existed, and I have made a lot of new friends along the way.

Helping trans friends: a lot of people struggle with the pronoun game. This is understandable; after all for years and years you've used i.e. 'he' to describe your friend and now she is asking to be called 'she'. It can take time to adjust. However, you should always respect your friend's choice. If you think it's hard, how hard do you think it is for your friend? Get on board with a new pronoun quickly and never EVER use the word 'it' or 'he/she'. That is NOT COOL.

N FOR NON-BINARY

Increasingly, people are rejecting traditional concepts of male and female. Perhaps we're *all* waking up to the idea that gender, largely, is a construct. Yes, some people think we are wholly defined by our biology and genes, but I think that steers us into some very bleak territory. As Chaz Bono once said, 'gender is between your ears, not your legs' and that's so true. As we can't know if being male *feels* one way and being female *feels* different (as we only have our individual experience to go on), all we can ever control is how we wish to express our personal identities. For some people, that's traditionally female, for some it's traditionally male, but for many, many people it's *neither* or *both*. Guess what? That's fine. 'Non-binary' or 'gender fluid' are becoming identities in their own right, and free people up to express their gender however they like. Miley Cyrus described herself as gender fluid in 2015, raising awareness further.

INTERSEX

Intersex is not so much an identity, in that you can't really choose it. (Remember, you can't choose your preference, but you can choose a label or identity.) Since intersex is used as a label, by both intersex people and doctors, it's worth mentioning here. A person is born intersex if they have genitalia or sexual characteristics that do not conform to strict definitions of male and/or female. This does NOT make them transgender, as they may agree with the gender they are assigned (most intersex people, rightly or wrongly, are assigned a sex at birth).

Transgender issues are linked with intersex issues, as many intersex people grow up to disagree with the gender they were assigned and seek to change.

WHAT IS CISGENDER?

Cisgender is basically the opposite of transgender. It simply means when your gender identity matches the identity you were given at birth. Therefore, the majority of people will identify as 'cis' even if they don't know it – it removes the need for anyone to say they are 'normal', which, as we said, is a manky word. Going back to my definition above, I am actually a gay cis man.

As a final word on all these identities, gay-rights activist Peter Tatchell says he looks forward to a day when all of these labels will be redundant and we can all just be human. I think I look forward to that day too.

However you identify, be it lesbian, gay, bisexual, trans, queer, asexual, curious or carrot, we all have something in common – we are a minority, and we have made brave steps to identify as such; a refusal to hide; a declaration of who we are. So label shop, label swap or don't wear one at all. Just be comfortable with YOU and let others wear whatever labels they like.

This first step, our self-acceptance, is by FAR the hardest step of the journey. The rest, this book can help with.

If you identify as straight, you should keep reading too. Frankly, LGBT* people need all the straight allies we can get, and you too can arm yourself with knowledge.

CHAPTER 3:
YOU CAN'T MISTAKE
OUR BIOLOGY

How old were you when you realised 'being gay' was a thing? Probably pretty young . . . five? Six? Seven? Now, how old were you when you asked the bigger question of WHY people are gay? There has to be a reason.

Before we examine some of the possible factors that made you who you are, I think it's important to state that IT DOESN'T MATTER. We don't need excuses for our existence, and I don't hear anyone asking heterosexual people, 'What made you straight?'

Remember High Priestess Gaga and *Born This Way*. Your sexuality or gender is as natural as your eye colour, and you should never be ashamed of it.

WARNING: THIS SECTION IS JAM-PACKED WITH ENOUGH GOBBLEDYGOOK TO STRETCH MY PITIFUL BIOLOGY A LEVEL TO BREAKING POINT. GET A CUP OF TEA AND PREPARE FOR SOME SCIENCE.

So what made us same-sex inclined or transgender? Well, don't hold your breath, because I'm afraid the boffins at the RuPaul Institute of Gay Heritage Technology (RIGHT) really can't come to anything resembling a definitive answer – more a collection of half-convincing theories.

Let's take a look at the most coherent, starting with sexuality.

1. TWIN STUDIES

Several studies have been carried out to show that identical twins have a much higher chance of BOTH being gay than do non-identical twins, suggesting that there is some sort of 'gay gene'. However, it is thought that gay twins are keen to volunteer for scientific studies, and this may have somewhat skewed the data.

2. CHROMOSOME LINKAGE

In the 1990s, there were various studies on the catchily named chromosome Xq28 – the so-called gay gene. In GAY MEN, this gene is passed down on the mother's side of the family, often seeming to explain why gay men may have gay brothers or gay uncles.

3. EPIGENETICS

Oh, it's only going to get more complicated, I'm afraid. After work surrounding Xq28 was somewhat discredited, scientists instead looked to 'epi-marks' as a possible explanation. I want you to imagine your mum and dad's genetic code (don't worry, I'm not going to ask you to imagine them bumping uglies). On some of our genes we have epi-marks. These are sort of like Post-it notes with added information for the gene's job. On the male chromosomes, it may have 'YO – YOU SHOULD LIKE GIRLS' written on it, while the female chromosomes may come with a note saying, 'YOU DEFINITELY WANT TO HAVE SEX WITH DUDES.' Now, for a long time it was assumed that these Post-its were removed before being passed via SWEATY PARENT SEX (sorry, couldn't resist) to their baby. But now scientists believe this isn't always the case and that sometimes these Post-it notes saying whom you're meant to fancy get 'stuck' onto the kids. So, in short, boys can get the epi-mark for liking boys from their mums, and girls can get the epi-mark for liking girls from their dads.

Tell them that they should freak out about your sexuality.

I imagine they'll enjoy being blamed.

4. MORE SCIENCY THEORIES

Having lots of brothers – With each boy baby, your mum's immune system gets better at blocking male hormones in the womb, making gay male babies more likely. (Note how a lot of studies have focused on gay men. Figures. The patriarchy.)

Pheromones – An area of men's (again men, I'm afraid) brains reacts differently to different scents depending on sexuality. Gay men's brains respond to locker-room sweat smell, while straight men respond to a compound found in lady-wee. Humans are gross.

Brain structure – Several studies have found that the hypothalamus part of the brain may be a little different in homosexual people. That said, they found this for the most part through poking about in sheep.

Prenatal hormones – Linked to the 'having lots of brothers' idea, this is the idea that the changes in brain structure possibly come from the levels of androgen that we are exposed to in the womb – it can change the 'gender' of our brain, including sexual attraction. Oh, OK.

Exotic becomes erotic

I like this one for no other reason than that it has a silly name. This idea states that our biology (brains, hormones, genes) predisposes us to like stuff associated with one gender more than the other. Eventually, we see those who are exotic (i.e. boys if we like girl stuff, girls if we're typically more masculine) as sexy.

I'm meant to be an impartial reporter of these theories, but this one seems like total bum. I mean, REALLY?

Evolutionary studies

Clearly, there are some issues with the idea of a 'gay gene'. Gay men and lesbians who had babies would produce gay babies, right? Wrong. Why are there so many gay people coming from straight parents?

From a Darwinian perspective, homosexuality makes no sense – if we were all gay, the human race would die out. Gay people (being less likely to now reproduce) remove themselves from the gene pool.

There have been several theories about this. One is that perhaps the gene predisposing people to homosexuality actually poses a benefit in heterosexual people (only sometimes making the person LGB*), and this is why the trait continues to be passed down through generations. Another theory is that gay uncles and aunts tend to dote more on their nieces or nephews, helping to ensure the youngsters' survival and in that way propagating their own genetic code.

Biological differences between gay and straight

- Gay men and straight women have equally proportioned brain hemispheres. Gay women and straight men have slightly larger right hemispheres.

- Gay men have slightly longer and thicker winkies. **Excellent.**

- The amygdala of gay men is more responsive to porn than those of straight men. So we have bigger dicks and we're hornier. Jus' sayin'.

- Finger length ratios may vary between lesbians and straight women. Get combing the streets with a finger ruler, ladies!

A problem I have

All of these theories seem to have us programmed to be GAY or STRAIGHT from before we were born. I find this very exclusive of bi, curious and queer people.

Clearly, biology is playing into our sexual preference – but not our lifestyle choices. No gene is going to help you come out, nor is it going to determine what kind of family situation you're born into. Therefore, environmental factors must play a huge role that shouldn't be overlooked.

I imagine a child born into a liberal, accepting family in the UK is far more likely to IDENTIFY as gay or lesbian than a child born into a strict Muslim family in Yemen. You get me?

Also, I doubt there's a gene for 'bored and horny' or 'feeling a bit experimental'. I worry that scientists don't take into account the fluidity or playfulness of sex and sexuality. My advice is to be interested and go 'Mmmm' when reading the theories in this chapter but to simply accept that when it comes to sexuality, IT IS HOW IT IS. And that's fine. Enjoy!

Biological explanations for Transgenderedness

For many decades, it was thought that being trans was a result of environmental or parental factors. However, the high-profile case of David Reimer (1965–2004) changed things somewhat. Born as a boy and called 'Bruce', Reimer was accidentally castrated in a botched circumcision and was raised as a girl. However, David ALWAYS identified as male, suggesting gender cannot be learned – our identity is born with us.

Modern scientists have found possible genetic causes for transgenderism: both male-to-female (MTF) and female-to-male (FTM) transsexuals have variations in hormone binding genes, while FTM transsexuals may also be lacking some female-only gene distribution patterns.

Other scientists have found variations in brain structure in both MTF and FTM transsexuals – in both cases, the test subjects have the typical brain patterns of their preferred gender identity.

Finally, and this is AMAZING, FTM transsexuals often report 'phantom limb syndrome' for a penis from childhood, and while cis men who have lost their members DO get phantom penis sensations, MTF patients do NOT. Mind-blowing stuff, right? GHOST WILLIES. (There's my next YA book sorted.)As with sexuality, I'm not big into biological determinism. We are all free to play with gender.

What have we learned?

OK, that was a whole lot of science. I hope you feel cleverer; I certainly do. I have summarised about a hundred experiments and studies over the previous five pages. There are tons and tons of research papers and books you can track down if you want more information on this – it is fascinating.

I think the important thing to take away from this chapter is that we have precious little control over our sexual desires or gender even if we do have control over our identity. However you choose to identify, though, no one can ever say your feelings are a choice. I'll say it again: when it comes to who you fancy or who you are, IT IS HOW IT IS and you never, ever have to apologise for this. You were born this way.

THINGS THAT DID NOT MAKE YOU GAY

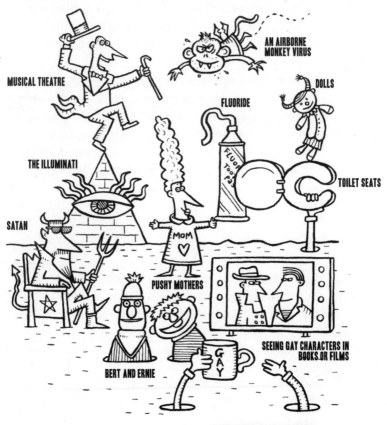

MUSICAL THEATRE

AN AIRBORNE MONKEY VIRUS

DOLLS

FLUORIDE

THE ILLUMINATI

TOILET SEATS

SATAN

MOM ♥

PUSHY MOTHERS

BERT AND ERNIE

GAY

SEEING GAY CHARACTERS IN BOOKS OR FILMS

SHARING MUGS WITH GAY PEOPLE

CHAPTER 4:
STEREOTYPES ARE POO

Aren't gay men BRILLIANT? They are such loyal friends and they're always good for a laugh. They're the BEST shopping partners too and are always up for dancing to Beyoncé! GBFs 4EVA!

Yes, dear, and all Irish people are leprechauns and Paris is full of onion-wearing mime artists.

Representation of LGBT* people in the media is getting BETTER, but it is still vastly limited. Unless you are one of the lucky people who grew up around gay people, you might think that all gay men are fabulously camp chat show presenters and all gay women are sports commentators. Hopefully, you recognise that this isn't the case. You can probably count the number of transgender people on TV on one hand.

LEGENDARY gay rights campaigner Harvey Milk encouraged all gay people to be more visible so that young people would be surrounded by a spectrum of infinitely varied gay people – that way people would see that stereotypes are meaningless.

Let's take a look at some common stereotypes about gay people.

STEREOTYPE	FACT OR FICTION?
All gay men dress like gods and dance like Fred Astaire.	Go to any gay club on a Saturday night and you'll see a sublime mixture of dad dancing, self-conscious shuffling and OTT arms-aloft raving. Some gay men dress well, and some dress like David Hasselhoff.
All gay women have short hair.	Yes. Gay women have a faulty version of the hair-growing gene. What do you think? Of course this isn't true! Lots of gay women have long hair, and straight women have short hair.
Gay men fancy kids.	Ah, this old chestnut. Some deeply homophobic people truly believe this is the case. Think about it – you know what gay men like? BIG, HAIRY BLOKES WITH BIG WILLIES. You know who have none of these attributes? Kids. Gay men like men – that's the whole point.
Gay men always work as cabin crew or hairdressers.	Some do. Most don't.
Gay women hate men.	I imagine they'd hate men who said that to them, yes.
Gay women are all desperate to have threesomes with men, just like in porn.	This feeds into the age-old misconception that all gay people are waiting for is the 'right guy/girl' to make them realise the error of their ways. Sorry, boys, but gay women get turned on by vaginas. And you don't have one.
Gay men are massive sluts.	Firstly, we don't use that word because it's not very nice. We'll discuss this in much more detail later, but CLEARLY this isn't true of all gay men.
All trans people are gay.	TWO DIFFERENT THINGS. If you draw a little Venn diagram, there will be a bit in the middle where the gay circle overlaps the trans circle, but that's true of anything, right?
Gay men all have HIV/AIDs.	Le sigh. Sadly, this is why a lot of older people are wary of gay men. This statement is WRONG on about fifty levels, all of which are potentially dangerous. We will discuss the AIDs pandemic and STIs in much more detail later because they ARE important to gay culture.
Gay women all have cats.	Yes. All of them. It's how they plan to conquer the world. A platoon of lesbians with armoured cats.*Sarcastic face*
Gay men are 'girls'.	Penis? Check! Yup, gay men are, in fact, male.
Bisexual people are 'hedging their bets'.	If this were the case, wouldn't we ALL do it?
Transsexual people are cross-dressers.	We discussed this in the section on being trans.
Transgender people are sick.	Sick to death of statements like that, yes.

I think you get the message – there are far, far too many stereotypes about LGBT* people.

WHY stereotypes are poo

'I think all stereotypes are sh*t. Whether it's a racial stereotype or a sexual stereotype or a cultural stereotype, you're always going to find SOMEONE who fits the bill. But stereotypes suggest that a group, or at least a majority of that group, behaves in a certain way, and that kills the idea of individuality.'

BFL, 43, Minnesota, USA.

Stereotypes are rubbish for one very simple reason – they dehumanise people and allow terrible prejudices and discrimination to come creeping in. Bigots THRIVE on stereotypes. It's much easier to hate a faceless stereotype than it is a human being.

As well as being awesome, LGBT* people are also a persecuted minority. This is not awesome. I'm afraid it's not all cocktail parties and gay cruises – for many people all around the world, being gay is ILLEGAL. I know, it's cray.

Let's think about some other persecuted minorities. I'm going to use an example we see in newspapers and on the telly a lot – Muslims. Instead of talking about 'terrorists', very often newsreaders talk about 'Muslim terrorists' or 'Muslim extremists'. Does it matter that the terrorists identify as Muslim? NO, IT DOES NOT. People who aren't very clever start to associate the two phrases until bigots start saying things like, 'All Muslims are terrorists.' This, my friend, is dangerous thinking.

Similarly, stereotypes about LGBT* people fuel homophobia, which we will talk about a lot more in the next chapter.

Each LGBT* person is completely unique and individual. Although a lot of gay people might like some of the same things (there is a rich and varied gay or queer 'culture'), no two LGBT* people are the same.

Even if you identify as gay, lesbian, bisexual, transgender or queer, you're still just you. There are infinite ways of being gay, and they're all brilliant. So saying things like, 'All gay men dress well,' is unhelpful and dehumanising to the gay men who don't give a flying fig about fashion.

Remember, being gay is just one element of your identity, so how could we possibly all be the same?

Which stereotypes bug you?

- I find the 'gay best friend' stereotype very grating.
  (R, 17, London)

- Lesbians as man-haters; bisexuals as promiscuous and/or secretly preferring men, or not existing; asexuals being non-existent; and all asexual people being prudes.
  (Nina, 16, UK)

- All gay men are promiscuous, bisexuals of all genders are promiscuous, black lesbians are always butch and aggressive, and feminine lesbians are bisexual really, trans people all have issues. (**Mica, 23, London**)

- The limp-wristed, fey, praying mantis stereotype. Don't get me wrong, I can bust out a cutting witticism like any self-respecting queen, but I'm still a bloke. (**Luke, 27, London**)

- Bisexuals are sluts, greedy, secretly gay, secretly straight, easy, faking it, cheaters, or getting the best of both worlds. (**Anon, 15**)

- Lesbians as butch or masculine. Like all people, we come in all shapes, sizes, ways of dress, etc. I hate being told that I can't be gay because I don't 'look like a lesbian'. Another one that gets me is that lesbians are good at fixing things, 'cause I sure as hell ain't!
(**Michelle, 23, USA**)

- The one that really bothers me is the assumption that all MTF trans people are perverts, transitioning to gain some kind of sexual thrill from their position. (**Laura, 21, UK**)

Subcultures vs. stereotypes

Every once in a blue moon, stereotypes may have the tiniest grain of truth (lots of gay men DO like Beyoncé, but who doesn't – she's the dancing Aslan of pop), but that doesn't mean it should be applied to a whole group! Except for the one about Parisian mimes. That's all true. KIDDING!

One of the best things about choosing to IDENTIFY as gay or bi is that you are already making your own rules. I'm not for a second suggesting there is one set of rules for straight people and one for non-straight, but identifying as LGB or T or * means you have opted out of the majority group (you're never too young to learn that the whole world is largely run and designed for straight, white, cis men, or 'the patriarchy'). This pretty much means you are free to adopt whichever elements of gay or queer culture you see fit.

The biggest bonus to coming out is that you can be who you want to be with no hiding and no apologies.

'[When I came out] it was easier, because I had been pretending to be something I wasn't. Being gay meant that I could be more honest about the things that I liked.'

Ben, 23, Manchester.

Basically, you can pick and choose which 'stereotypes' you want to adhere to, because some of them are part of a great tradition set out by generations of LGB* people. What if you DO want to work as cabin crew? Do it. What if you want to work as cabin crew AND play rugby AND listen to musical theatre soundtracks BUT ALSO thrash metal? Well, guess what? Your identity is yours to design.

If you're a gay girl who wants to shave her head, who the heck has any right to tell you not to? It's your hair.

I'd like to point out that gay people do not cause homophobia with our behaviour. Homophobes are simply bigoted, and that, my friend, is their problem.

LGB* people do not choose to be LGB*. Homophobes choose to hate.

There are various threads to gay culture which are not stereotypes, but are rather identities within an identity. You can't choose whether you fancy guys or girls, but once you've accepted who you fancy, there ARE lifestyle choices to be made. These are some of the various subcultures you may have heard about or may experience on the gay scene:

BEARS

This refers to big, hairy gay men, often with beards.

OTTERS

SLIMMER hairy guys with beards. I'm not making this up, seriously.

CUBS

Not surprisingly, these are YOUNGER big hairy gay men, often with beards.

TWINKS

This one is for the boys again. A twink is usually a young, hairless gay man. Waxing strips at the ready!

MUSCLE MARY

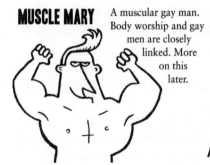

A muscular gay man. Body worship and gay men are closely linked. More on this later.

BUTCH DYKE

This refers to a gay woman who has adopted some traditionally male characteristics (e.g. a moustache) but doesn't identify as male. Remember, it's only OK to use the term 'dyke' if you're describing yourself.

SCALLIES

Usually a gay guy with a penchant for sportswear and man jewellery.

FEM/LIPSTICK LESBIAN

A gay woman who enjoys 'traditionally female' dress, hair and make-up (although what does THAT mean?).

Of course, most gay men and women are NONE of those things and are just men or women who fancy people with the same genitals as them. It's an identity buffet – you can take your plate up and just have a little scoop of gay, or you can go nuts and load up on as many labels as you can carry back to the table.

'I sometimes think it would be easier if I did look more like a stereotypical "lesbian", because it would be easier to pull! But that's just not me ... you have to wear the clothes you like.'

Jenny, 31, Dublin, Ireland.

If you identify as lesbian or gay, I bet you think you're pretty good at being able to spot a fellow 'mo, right? I'd like you to take a pen and in the space below draw a gay man and a gay woman . . . GO!

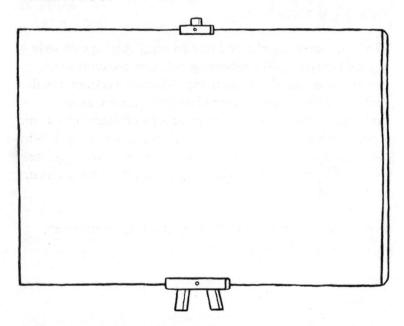

I bet some of you have drawn either:

this   or maybe
             or this   this

But for many decades, LGBT* people had to be INVISIBLE for fear of persecution. Therefore, most gay men and women had to blend in effortlessly like alien bodysnatchers – only not evil, obviously. It's super homophobic to suggest that all gay men and women look alike.

That said, some gay men and women enjoy playing with style and gender typing. Any subculture will have uniforms to an extent – look at goths or mods, etc. Adopting a certain sexual-identity look is very different to being transgender, as we discussed in the section on identity. It is more about an aesthetic – borrowing gender norms or aspiring towards androgyny. Why shouldn't a woman cut her hair short? Why shouldn't guys wear make-up? Part of the fun of being gay is sticking two fingers up at 'the norm'.

In the next section, let's look at some particular stereotypes, starting with gay men.

CAMP

The word 'camp' is often applied to gay men, although anything can be camp. Gay women can be fantastically camp – just look at Sue Perkins. Camp means excessive, flamboyant, kitsch and theatrical but also sophisticated, witty and subversive behaviour or things. Later on, when we look at 'gay icons', you'll see that many celebrities beloved by gay people possess these qualities.

Despite 'camp' sounding literally fabulous, it is more often than not used as an insult, sometimes by straight people but, perhaps more shockingly, by gay people themselves. 'He's too camp for me' trips off the tongue of many a gay guy when he's deciding whether or not to bum someone.

Another term we could have added to the definition of camp is 'effeminate', and this is where the problem seems to be.

It seems unlikely that young gay men are born camp and yet, when I was a teacher, there were glaringly camp five- and six-year-olds in my Year 1 classes. How can this be? One possibility is that these boys identify as female from a young age – lots of trans people do; remember Rory's story. Maybe they're sexually confused, meaning that they are attracted to other boys but are unaware that being gay is an option, so they start to echo 'female' traits. However, this could be as a result of their feeling 'different' to their male peers, so they simply adopt the traits of their closer female friends. Another theory is that young gay men have a refined eye for camp and track down camp icons in the media and emulate their behaviour.

Whatever the origin of camp, it's fair to say that however butch gay men think they are, total strangers are often MORE than able to spot a gay chap at twenty paces, especially if they themselves are gay.

If we were to ask a hundred gay men, 'Do you think you're camp?' though, they'd scratch their testicles, adopt a tone ten decibels lower than normal and say, 'Naaaarrr, mate, not me.' I estimate possibly three or four might say, 'Oooh, sometimes, if I've had a drink.'

Gay men seem terrified of being camp. They plaster their Grindr profiles with 'Straight Acting' and frantically grow beards. (More on hyper-masculinity in a moment.) The consensus seems to be that, while we think camp is great for chat show hosts, we don't wanna bum it.

Is this simply roaring misogyny? Do gay men just hate women and anything stereotypically female? Living in a male-dominated world seems to have infected us with a notion that anything male is BETTER. Is this why some gay women ALSO reject feminine norms and chase down the characteristics of the dominant group on the planet – men?

I don't think so. I think it's far worse. I think we hate OURSELVES.

Bummer, right?

But this isn't our fault. After DECADES of being told in all sorts of ways that gay men are LESS THAN straight men, we've turned that hate inwards. We aren't rejecting female traits; we're rejecting stereotypically gay ones.

How sad is this? Answer: Mega sad.

We might not all like all of our stereotypes, but they are ours. They belong to us. The rest of the world is so shady about gay people that, love it or hate it, I think we could all be a little bit more supportive of gay culture. Let me tell you something, boys and girls, you can 'straight act' all you want, but if you're sleeping with your own sex, to the rest of the world you're as gay as John Waters living in a pink tent with Clare Balding while watching *Drag Race*.

You might as well own it.

DESPERATE DANS

As mentioned previously, any subculture may develop a uniform, but for some gay men the 'look' has gone far beyond mere clothing. It's – you guessed it – a stereotype, but gay men are often thought to have the best bodies on the market.

Go to any big gay club and – another stereotype incoming– you'll see HUGE guys shuffling around with their tops off. Barrel chests, six-packs and necks as big as my thigh have become a curious norm. It seems the aspirational aesthetic is that of CARTOON HUMAN Desperate Dan.

There are couple of theories behind this gym-bunny culture. It could be linked to the gay man's love of all things masculine. Men want to shag men, so the more man there is of you, the better. If you want to get laid a lot, be a fantasy . . . be a cartoon. Be the opposite of feminine.

The second theory is sadder. If a young gay guy is being drip fed messages that female < male and gay < straight, then gay guys may develop an internal loathing of all things female and gay, thus striving for the most masculine appearance possible – like you can pump your way out of being gay.

The Velvet Rage author Alan Downs supports the notion that the gay obsession with body mass is down to self-loathing. He believes gay men chase impossible levels of fitness to overcome an inner sadness – you'll be happy if only you become that bit more perfect and if just a few more men want to bum you. He believes gay men look for validation in all the wrong places.

I don't wholly agree with either of those theories. I simply think we're subjected to peer pressure, even as adults – we see a Muscle Mary in porn, in the club, on the beach and start to think it's achievable. This is something that women have been subject to for years, particularly from exposure to six-foot, six-stone models in fashion magazines.

It's a statistical fact that gay men are more prone to eating disorders than our straight brothers. We're going to extreme lengths to fit in down the clubs. Given that I've never seen a straight guy dancing with his shirt off, it's not a mystery to figure out why.

Clue: A six pack never made anyone happy. No-one ever got to the stage at the gym where they said, 'I DID IT! I AM NOW SATISFIED.' Maybe some of us get hooked on the idea that true happiness is just one gym session away and so we keep going.

As I said in the section on camp, it doesn't matter what you look like or how you dress, once you're gay, you're gay in the eyes of the world. There is no **'he's gayer than me'**. If you find yourself saying things like that, we're dealing with something very sad and very deep rooted.

STEROIDS

Desperate Dan bodies are also no great enigma. STEROIDS. I'm afraid it's that simple. Go to a gay beach and play REAL OR STEROIDS? Some guys have naturally lean, defined or even muscled bodies, but I think you can spot a steroid user a mile off. Steroid use is endemic on the gay scene. All those really huge guys, with few exceptions, are using.

So. Let's talk about the 'roids. The ones we're talking about are anabolic-androgenic steroids (or AAS for short). Users inject or swallow high doses of the male hormone testosterone, which promotes growth. Most users take them non-continuously, causing fluctuations in their body mass as and when they need to look buff. Some users take a cocktail of different steroids, a practice known as 'stacking'.

If everyone's on them, they can't be so bad, right?
Right? Wrong.

BENEFITS	For the **duration you take the hormone,** you will get bigger, especially if usage is combined with a stringent gym routine.
SIDE EFFECTS	**Mental/Behavioural:** Aggression * Mood swings * Paranoia * Mania * Delusions * Depression * Suicidal thoughts * Reduced sex drive * Insomnia
	Physical: Enlarging of the heart * Heart attack * Liver damage Severe acne * Fluid retention * Testicular shrinkage Low sperm count * Baldness * Increased risk of prostate cancer * Risk of HIV and hepatitis through needle use

I think that table speaks for itself. As with any illegal drug (note that some people are prescribed hormone treatment for valid reasons), **just because your mates are doing it doesn't mean it's safe.**

Also, I'm not sure how I can say this delicately. NO ONE WANTS TO SHAG A BALD SPOTTY PSYCHO WITH BALLS LIKE SHRIVELLED RAISINS. (I'm known for my tact.)

So it's a vicious circle. Guys will only look buff for as long as they're on the drugs, so you are well aware your physique is not down to you or your efforts at the gym – like fake self-esteem. Frankly, it's cheating, pure and simple.

More to the point, no one ever made themselves happy just by going to the gym. The big guys still wanna be bigger. It's a never-ending quest for a state of perfection that doesn't exist. Guys on steroids aren't happier, they're just bigger. Finally, the Desperate Dan look is very specific, and not everyone is into that 'roidy look (I think it looks FREAKISH). It's no guarantee of finding a love match.

```
'You can tell when a guy's on steroids - bulging head
veins! I personally think it's not such a great look.
Huge, great arms and chests with skinny little legs. I
find it repulsive, to be honest.'

T, 22, Brisbane, Australia.
```

GIRL WARS

While gay men wage war against camp with muscle, gay women have their own in-fights. This war is about femininity. 'Butch dykes' often take issue with 'lipstick lesbians' and vice versa. You hear a lot of arguments like this:

'I'm a lesbian so I want a woman who actually looks like a woman.' Or 'She's just pretending to be dead femme; she's really a dyke.'

As with gay men, this infighting isn't helping anyone – we get enough grief from outside the community as it is. It seems that some women feel that adhering to or avoiding stereotypes is somehow damaging 'the cause', but of course this isn't true. All any person can be is comfortable. It's all about personal taste. Some women like make-up and fashion, and some don't.

You'll notice that THIS HAS NOTHING TO DO WITH SEXUALITY. In fact, what is more troubling is that straight women might be accused of being gay purely because they don't like fussing over their hair, clothes and make-up – that's both homophobic AND sexist.

What's more, when it comes to dating, some women are very into butch lesbians, some women are into girly girls – there really is something for everyone.

MAN-HATERS

A mixture of poor media representation and sheer misogyny has also furthered the myth of the 'angry lesbian', the idea that all gay women are militants who seek to kill and scalp men. This response is identical to the one that women get from men when they use the word 'feminism'. It's a way of men putting women down – to keep them in their place. Note that feminists are often accused of being lesbians. Let's get it straight. Gay women do not hate men. They simply don't want to have sex with them.

Very often, when talking about women's issues, I find the term 'men' is used to describe 'the patriarchy'. This is also a mistake.

'JOIN US'

This is so ridiculous it hardly warrants air time, but pornography (more on that later) has led some young heterosexual men to think that scantily clad gay women will coquettishly beckon them into a soft-focus three-way. Clearly this is not the case.

Some bi or queer women probably are looking for threesomes with clammy-palmed internet men, but most aren't. No lesbian women are. I can't state this enough: Lesbians like vaginas. They don't even want blokes watching. I KNOW, how INCONSIDERATE. Note the sarcastic tone.

There is a more serious side to the idea that gay women are 'waiting for the right man'. In certain parts of South Africa, 'corrective rape' is a terrible, heart-breaking practice whereby gay women (as many as an estimated ten a week) are raped or gang-raped 'for their own good' to turn them heterosexual. All of us, straight, gay or otherwise must, MUST accept that women of all sexualities have the same sexual freedoms as men.

GAY VS. LESBIAN

One of the strangest stereotypes about us is that gay men hate lesbians and vice versa. Imma save you some time. If you are chatting to gay men who are dismissive of lesbians (or for that matter disparaging of the vagina as a concept), you are talking to misogynist dicks. If you are talking to a gay woman who classifies all gay men as lesbian haters, you are talking to a sexist homophobe.

It works both ways.

Needless to say, gay people often show a startling lack of awareness about trans people – confusing drag queens and transgendered people constantly.

There is no reason for these conflicts beyond trashy, worn, flea-bitten, drag-show stand-up jokes that should have been thrown out with crimpers and Tamagotchis.

Again, there is so much homophobia in the world. Why on earth would we want to add to it?

OUT IN THE COLD

Poor bisexual people. I'll include queer, pan and curious people in this section too. Because as humans we're trained to enjoy binary things, people not conforming to GAY OR STRAIGHT can often be rejected by both sides.

Straight people think bisexuals are 'greedy' or 'indecisive', while gay people lean towards, 'Oh they must be gay.' Both think that, 'when they meet the right person they'll pick a team.' As I said before, I really don't think bisexual people would bother hedging their bets. It would be so much EASIER to pick a side, I'd imagine. Therefore, it takes guts to identify this way.

It's up to you to decide if bi people are getting the best or worst of both worlds. I'd argue that bisexual people aren't getting any of the privileges of straight society while they're also lacking the community of being gay or lesbian.

Let's all hug a bisexual this week. They need our support too.

CONFORMITY

In any group, there are bound to be social norms, and being LGBT* is no different. Perhaps some stereotypes arose from these shared attributes. No one has to conform to these traits, however. Despite the hundreds of stereotypes we've talked about in this chapter – regarding hairstyles, clothes, behaviour – it's important to remember that even if you DO conform to certain stereotypes, you are still an individual. There is only one you, and you can do whatever you like as long as you look after yourself and don't hurt anyone else.

Who do you want to be? There's only one rule: always be true to yourself.

CHAPTER 5:
THE FEAR

So far I hope I've sold this LGBT* thing pretty well. I mean, it does sound brilliant, doesn't it? You get to dress how you like and make out with whomever you want. It's dead hip and trendy (just ask Zachary Quinto, Andrej Pejic or Angel Haze). You get to be part of an avant-garde subculture with links to art, music and fashion. But, most importantly, you will be at one with who you really are. You are finally you.

HURRAH!

Ah, if only it were that simple. While some people glide effortlessly out of the closet like prized figure skaters, others find the process more akin to Bambi learning to walk. For some, coming to terms with their sexuality and coming out is the hardest thing they will ever do.

But why is it so hard for some people?

HOMOPHOBIA/TRANSPHOBIA

Homophobia is described in the Merriam-Webster dictionary as the 'irrational fear of, aversion to, or discrimination against homosexuality or homosexuals.' Note the 'irrational' part. The definition is also true of transphobia.

Homophobia, broadly speaking, comes from two places – inside and out: other people airing anti-gay sentiments, but also individuals themselves believing that there's something wrong with being gay or bi. Again, the same is true of transphobia. Many trans people will have grown up in environments where they have been led to believe there is something 'weird' about swapping gender.

What if you believe there's something wrong with being gay, bi or trans *and* you happen to BE gay, bi or trans. This is more common than you might think. For ease, let's call this SELF-LOATHING.

If a young person thinks there is something wrong with being LGBT*, they're hardly likely to sing their identity from a balcony, Evita style, while waving a rainbow flag, are they?

Clearly, the issue here is **why do they think being LGBT* is wrong?** I can't imagine anyone is born homophobic (or transphobic), so it must come from external sources, which brings us neatly to homophobia.

EXPLICIT HOMOPHOBIA

Sadly, there are small-minded bigots everywhere, and they don't half enjoy letting you know how idiotic they are. 'It's a free country,' they say. 'I can say what I like.' Well, actually, inciting hatred is a criminal offence so, no, you can't.

- Some homophobes hate gay people because they think it's a part of their faith – we'll deal with that in chapter 6.

- Some homophobes think it's dirty or disgusting. *Eye roll*

- Some homophobes think that gay people will crawl down their chimneys and somehow convert them like GAY VAMPIRES.

See? Irrational. Also stubborn, ill-informed and ignorant.

A: straight

Transphobic people will be similarly disgusted with trans people, whether they think it's just an impossibility for one to change their gender or if, as with gay people, they see trans people as EVIL SEX SIRENS WHO WILL FOOL YOU WITH THEIR GENDER SECRET. Talk to a certain type of cisgender person about Thailand and within seconds they'll say something disparaging about the third gender, I promise you. Jerry Springer was terrible for this too.

If a young person has grown up with parents or carers who have tutted every time a gay couple

pops up in a soap opera, they have sent a unanimous message to their child that they do not approve of LGBT* people. It doesn't even have to be parents or carers. If a peer group at school has spent ten years saying, 'HA! THAT PENCIL CASE IS WELL GAY!' the same message is being spread: that pencil case is rubbish, and so are you.

THIS IS WHY WE MUST NEVER USE 'GAY' AS A DEROGATORY TERM. EVER.

B : LGBT

The language we use is incredibly powerful and oh-so-easy to internalise. I'd like you to do a little activity. You will need a pen or a pencil. On these pages are two (genderless) people. Keeping inside the lines (we're not animals), write all the words (both kind and unkind) you know that describe straight people in Person A and LGBT* people in Person B.

All done? I'm willing to bet that there's a lot more writing on Person B. Perhaps you've written 'straight', 'cis' or 'normal' on the Person A.

With the possible exception of 'breeder', there aren't an awful lot of derogatory terms about straight people, because our society is run predominantly by them.

However, Person B, I'd imagine, is covered from head to toe in abusive, offensive, ill-informed and damaging slurs. Am I right? Pretty much any words other than 'gay', 'lesbian', 'bi', 'transgender', 'queer' or 'curious' are inappropriate. This is why I personally won't list them in this book – I don't want to add to that toxicity. The words change, but there will always be brutal words to cut minority groups down to size. We call this an 'obliteration exercise'. Poor Person B is quite literally obliterated by insults.

There is no person left at all.

This is what homophobia does to young people. However thick our skin is, I imagine even the toughest young LGBT* person has thought, 'Oh, God, this isn't going to be easy.' And it isn't. Ever. Although we may be pleased we've figured ourselves out AND we may have the most supportive parents or carers in the universe, we all KNOW we're coming out into a world that is littered with hatefulness.

BUT it's this adversity that makes LGBT* people strong. It's why we call ourselves proud. If you can recognise how much hate there is in the world and still come out as LGBT*, you, my friend, are a fighter.

LGBT* people are STRONG. Because we have to be.

INSTITUTIONAL HOMOPHOBIA/ TRANSPHOBIA

This is a far more insidious type of homophobia. In fact, some people would say this isn't homophobia at all, but I think it's just as damaging.

I'd like you to pick up any magazine that isn't *Attitude*, *Diva* or *GT*. Have you done that? Good. Have a flick through and stick a Post-it note on any advertisements unambiguously featuring gay couples (i.e. not just two women laughing at salads).

Hint: You won't need ANY Post-it notes because there aren't going to be **ANY**.

We could have carried out similar tests at the cinema, on TV, in literature or at the theatre. With the possible exception of androgynous models like Andrej Pejic, Athena Wilson and Casey Legler, you're not going to see proper representation of trans people either.

Despite an AWFUL LOT of people in the world being LGBT*, we are practically invisible in the media, something I find BAFFLING given that white gay men are hugely OVER represented in media production.

Heteronormative values are forced down our throats from birth. Cinderella gets together with a dude she met once and lied to; the Little Mermaid rejects her entire culture for a bloke; that Princess trick even goes for a spot of bestiality and makes out with a FROG – but there are NO LGBT* role models for kids.

It doesn't get much better in TV, books and films. With a few notable exceptions (*And Tango Makes Three*, *The Family Book*), preschool and tween content is almost exclusively straight. What's more surprising is that content aimed at teens isn't entirely balanced. Some teen soap operas bravely include LGBT* characters (let's name UK soap *Hollyoaks* as an outstanding provider of LGBT* characters), and some authors (ahem) do feature LGBT* characters in their novels. However, the number of gay characters probably doesn't match the proportion of LGBT* teens in the real world, and too often LGBT* characters are suicidal runaways – hardly representative.

Outside of the media, let's talk about schools. In history, did you learn about Alan Turing? Harvey Milk? What about Billie Jean King?

What does this all mean? Why is this homophobia? Because every time you access a media outlet (including the Internet – I get straight singles ads on Facebook) or walk into school, you are being told

STRAIGHT = NORMAL.

So just because something isn't being openly hostile towards LGBT* people doesn't mean it's not quietly whispering that you're weird. Well, of course, you're FINE. It's the system that's total slug poop.

BEARD (noun)

A pretty woman attached to the arm of a closeted gay man to convince the rest of the world he is a straight, manly man, hence 'beard'.

Often to be found attached to the arms of closeted gay Hollywood actors such as NAMES REDACTED.

LAVENDER MARRIAGE (noun)

A fake marriage designed to make husband, wife or both appear heterosexual in the public eye. Popular in Hollywood with the likes of NAMES REDACTED, in seemingly happy marriages.

Both of these institutions deprive young LGBT* people of high-profile role models within Hollywood.

PARANOIA

Some would argue that both homophobia and transphobia have roots in suspicion and paranoia. The less we understand a group in society – the less we bother to learn – the more misconceptions and worries we have. For a long time, LGBT* people were relatively secretive, thus adding to the suspicion.

There was another major turning point, historically, that contributed to fear and paranoia, particularly about gay men, and that was the AIDS epidemic in the 1980s.

Let's have a history lesson:

The precise origin of HIV (human immunodeficiency virus) and AIDS (acquired immune deficiency syndrome) isn't known, although we can probably assume that the HIV infection, which attacks the immune system, jumped from apes to humans in Africa in the early twentieth century. Somehow, an unknown carrier of the virus travelled to the United States in the late 1970s, and the epidemic – and later pandemic – took hold.

For a time, HIV/AIDS was called GRID (gay-related immune deficiency), and by the time the medical world cottoned on to the fact that the illness could affect anyone – gay or not – the damage was already done. HIV/AIDS had become a 'gay disease'.

The reputation rose out of large gay communities in New York and California, where gay and bi men, who previously had no pressing need to use condoms, spread the infection at an alarming rate. Thousands of men died before clinicians could properly understand the disease.

Carriers of HIV were infected for years before becoming ill, and they infected others before they even realised they were carrying the virus. As they travelled the world, AIDS became a truly global problem, affecting EVERYONE, but the reputation of its being a 'gay thing' stuck.

Ask ANY gay person who grew up in the 1980s, and they will tell you about a terrifying TV advert that featured people being squashed by a giant AIDS gravestone. It caused national panic. The problem was that people didn't properly understand the disease. Some people thought that you could be infected by sharing mugs or toilet seats with carriers of the virus. You can't, obviously – the virus is transmitted mostly through blood and semen – but ignoramuses became very wary of gay people. This wasn't just about, 'they might try to trick me into bum sex,' any more, it was more, 'this person could kill me'.

It has taken thirty years to better educate people about HIV/AIDS, and there are now effective treatments but the stigma remains. Many out and proud gay men (and in this case, it IS mostly gay or bi men, not lesbians) will happily come out as gay but not as HIV positive for fear of judgement.

So for many awful, small-minded people, fear of gay people and fear of HIV/AIDS are permanently linked. Even if you're a child of the nineties, your parents will vividly remember the AIDS crisis. It's knowing their parents may still worry about HIV/AIDS that keeps a lot of young gay men, in particular, trapped at the back of the closet with a mouldy cagoule and some mothballs.

HOMOPHOBIC/TRANSPHOBIC BULLYING

Bullying is systematic abuse – verbal, physical or mental. Homophobia (as discussed) is the irrational fear of LGB* people. Put them together, and you have people being bullied for their sexuality. Transphobic bullying is aimed at people perceived to be transgender.

If we're being picky, someone screaming, 'Oi, woofter!' at you in a street isn't homophobic bullying, it's homophobic abuse. There's a key difference – bullying suggests a repeated campaign against an individual or group.

Let's start with **physical abuse or bullying.** Well, assault is always a crime, so the law is on your side. What's more, the Criminal Justice Act (2003) means that homophobic/transphobic crimes are dealt with more seriously and perpetrators given longer jail sentences. Some police forces also have an LGBT* liaison officer to help victims of crime. If you have been assaulted, you should call 999 or visit your local police station. If an assault happens in a school, it is still assault and you should call the police or get someone at your school to do so.

Third-party reporting – where you can get someone you know to report a crime – means you don't even have to identify yourself if you would rather keep your sexuality a secret.

Bullying in School

'When I was in Year 9, I came out and told my friends and they were OK with it, and then I told my dad. I asked if there was any support at school because I was being bullied. People used to pick on me, and one time a load of guys in a corridor stood up against the wall and said, "Cover your arses." I told the teachers I was getting bullied and I went to the student counsellor. After I spoke to her, she did a presentation about homophobic bullying. She got me to

speak to everyone about it, which was really
difficult. After the assembly . . . most of the bullies
stopped; only a few carried on. People still come up to
me and say how I was so brave.'

N, 17, Burgess Hill.

HOW TO CHALLENGE HOMOPHOBIC LANGUAGE

'THAT'S SO GAY' and 'NO HOMO' are still used way too often in
schools. What can you do if you hear it? A **QUIFF** system:

- Question: 'What do you mean by that?'

- Understanding: 'Do you know what "gay" actually means?'

- Institution: 'This school is a tolerant place; you can't say that.'

- Feel: 'I consider that offensive and homophobic.'

- Funny: 'Oh, wow, you're right, those shoes DO love each other
  even though they're both female.'

You should only challenge homophobic or transphobic language if it
is safe to do so – don't get into fights or put yourself at risk.

Homophobic and transphobic bullying is still a huge problem in
schools. Why? If you asked most young people, 'Do you hate
gay people?' they'd probably say no. I think it's because ALL
bullying is a problem in schools, and in such close quarters
people will lash out in any way they can – so whether it's your
hair, your weight, your glasses, your braces, your clothes OR

your perceived sexuality, people will always find something to take the piss out of.

THAT DOESN'T MAKE IT OK.

You can, of course, do your bit by not taking the piss out of other people. I don't think anyone is blameless when it comes to high school bullying. I think, on any given day, an individual can be both a bully and a victim.

Note how I said PERCEIVED sexuality. Remember, it's not just LGB* people who experience homophobic bullying – plenty of straight people have homophobic slurs made against them too.

The impact of homophobic bullying is huge. Gay rights charity Stonewall conducted research and found that fifty per cent of young LGB* students had truanted, while seventy per cent said it had affected their attainment at school. Well, that's just not good enough.

Homophobic and transphobic bullying can take many forms:

- Verbal abuse (name-calling)

- Rumour spreading

- Exclusion (being left out of stuff)

- Cyber bullying (online or text messages)

- Death threats

- Physical violence

- Sexual assault

The law is on your side again. BY LAW a school has to tackle all forms of bullying AND provide a safe space. Schools must also take POSITIVE steps to make young LGBT* people feel included – it's not enough for schools to merely tolerate us.

Be a SQUEAKY GATE: If you politely make enough noise at school, someone will eventually oil the hinges.

DOUGLAS'S STORY

In 2008, I moved back to Scotland after having lived abroad - a sixteen-year-old with my mind set on going to university in two years' time.

'Aye, see that new boy from Canada? F**kin' poof.'

What Kyle had said to Graeme in the corridor, oblivious to my presence, stuck with me. How did he know? I thought. Where has all this come from? I barely know him!

Having spoken to me once previously, he had made all of the assumptions he needed to start a two-year campaign of fear and isolation in my final years at high school. I could put it down to his immaturity - he was a year younger than me - but that only washes

so many times. There were outright verbal attacks and
a few physical attacks in PE by Kyle and Graeme.
Trying to explain why you've got massive bruises down
your side from being hit repeatedly with hockey
sticks isn't easy to do. Somehow, I managed to explain
it away.

I must admit, I look back at what happened and scream
at my naivety for not having said anything sooner. In
my last class on a Friday, I was discussing with a
friend whom I had told I was gay what our plans for
the weekend were. The plans involved seeing my then
boyfriend on Saturday for one thing or another.

'It's so nice', said Gemma, 'that you've managed to find
yourself a boyfriend.'

To my shock and total terror a girl who sat behind me
exclaimed, 'You're gay?! I would never have guessed!'

This would have been bearable, but there were two
problems: first being that my entire French class now
knew, and the second that Kyle sat directly behind
her. The last fifteen minutes of the class dragged on,
and I can't remember much apart from my overwhelming
sense of guilt, shame and excruciating lack of hubris;
people were demonising and defending me all at once.
Kyle finally had his confirmation: Douglas is gay.

I remember leaving early to collect my instruments
from the music department and scurrying to my locker.

By the time the rest of my year were down at the lockers, everyone knew. Some people were supportive, but Kyle, Graeme and their friends took great delight in tormenting me as I gathered my things together.

I didn't want to return to school on Monday. I was deliberately late so as not to have to deal with anyone in registration. By this point, my guidance teacher had a log of any incidents I had reported to her.

A few weeks later, I was standing at my local train station waiting for a taxi to take me home. (I didn't and still do not feel safe walking home at night on my own.) Kyle and Graeme walked past me and started shouting abuse at me in the street. I had learned to deal with it in school but not in the street. They left and I got in a taxi. When I was finally in my house and safe, I cried. Why me? How could they find this acceptable? As far as I could make out, it was my bedroom practices they were ridiculing, but somehow they'd cut to the very core of my identity.

How to tackle homophobic/transphobic bullying at school

These steps would work well for any kind of bullying:

- If you feel you're being victimised, start a journal. Not like, 'Dear Diary, he's so dreamy . . .' – more like names, dates, times and places. List reliable witnesses to the incident(s).

- This is the tough part. Tell someone you trust and show them your journal.

I KNOW – if you tell someone, it'll only get worse, right? WRONG. That is what people rely on to control you. Bullying is all about power and control. If you play along with what your aggressor wants, you are giving them all the power.

Your journal (and witnesses) will be very hard to argue with. A lot of young people think they won't be believed. YOU WILL. If the first teacher is unresponsive, go over their head. Find someone who will listen. Again, you're in control.

- Teachers are also under scrutiny. NO teacher or school wants to be perceived as homophobic or transphobic – their job or reputation would be on the line. They WILL help you.

- If you have been physically or sexually assaulted, you should call the police.

- What will happen next? Well, it depends on the school and the circumstances. By law, they have to act. I'm not gonna lie – the situation probably won't go away; but if you persist, your school will have to take tougher and tougher action to provide a safe space for you.

My advice is NEVER TAKE IT. As hard as it is, FIGHT.

As a final word on bullying, be aware that the day you leave school, your life as a young LGBT* person will improve, but only because everyone's life improves when they leave school.

It's become the slogan of the anti-homophobic-bullying movement, but IT GETS BETTER.

DISCRIMINATION IN THE WORKPLACE

'About a year in [to my MTF transition], six months after I started presenting as myself full-time, my employer, which had seemed understanding at first, took steps towards showing me the door. I wound up saving them the legal hassle and just quitting, because it was getting unbearable. There is essentially no protection, and you are definitely going to change jobs at some point, either because they fire you or because they make things very unpleasant until you leave voluntarily. As an example of unpleasantness, it's also fairly common (as happened to me) that they'll ask you to limit your bathroom usage to a single-occupancy facility if they have one; in my case, the only one available was an elevator ride away and badly ventilated, so it smelled horrible, unlike the normal facilities in that building. I also know several trans women who are required by their employers to use the men's room.'

Irene, 33, New Jersey, USA

But what if life doesn't improve once you head into the working world? As discussed, there are small-minded people everywhere, I'm afraid – in your office, your hospital, your police station, anywhere you can imagine. But more good news! Once again the law is on your side: being LGBT* is a 'protected characteristic' (which I like because it makes us sound like a beautiful rare butterfly on the verge of extinction in Java or something). It means, legally, that you cannot be discriminated against when applying for a job, in education, when buying or renting property, or when accessing public services (e.g. doctors or dentists).

Once you have a job, you cannot be dismissed because you're LGBT*; get less pay than a straight, cisgender colleague; be held back for promotion; or be made redundant (because you're LGBT*). If you're just plain crap at your job, then you're on your own, obviously.

If you think you have been discriminated against in the workplace, you can speak to your human resources department (if you have one) or get mediation from an outside agency such as ACAS (see the 'Helpful websites and numbers and stuff' section for contact details). You can also go to your local Citizens Advice Bureau. These sorts of disputes are often settled in court.

No Laughing Matter

Earlier, I said that it wasn't all Kylie and canapés, and I wasn't kidding. Homophobia kills. The following statistics are REAL and are why we all have to stand up against hate.

- One in six LGB people in the UK has experienced a hate crime or incident in the past three years.

- Young LGB people who are bullied are at a higher risk of suicide, self-harm and depression. Forty-one per cent have attempted or thought about taking their own life directly because of bullying, and the same number say that they deliberately self-harm directly because of bullying.

- Forty-nine per cent of lesbian and bisexual girls report symptoms consistent with depression, compared with twenty-nine per cent of gay and bisexual boys.

- One in seven gay and bisexual men (thirteen per cent) report moderate to severe depression, compared with seven per cent for the general population.

- Seventy-nine per cent of lesbian and bisexual women report a spell of sadness, misery or depression within the past year.

- Within the past year, one in fourteen gay or bi men has harmed himself on purpose. This rises to one in five for gay or bi women.

- Young LGBT people are 190 per cent more likely to misuse drugs and alcohol compared to straight youths. (University of Pittsburgh 2008)

Except where stated, all statistics courtesy of 'Stonewall – School Report 2012', 'Gay and Bisexual Men's Mental Health Survey 2011', 'Homophobic Hate Crime: The Gay British Crime Survey 2013'.

BOOM!

That was a maudlin bomb detonating in your face. Yeah, I
know this all makes for hugely depressing reading, but I'm all
about the TRUTH. Clearly, being LGBT* does not
automatically make you depressed or suicidal, but the fact is
that young LGBT* people, when exposed to hatred or
homophobia or when living with anxiety and threat, are bound
to be vulnerable to mental health problems.

This is why all of us – all LGBT* people, young and old – are
still working for greater acceptance and challenging
homophobia. Even a book like this would have been
unthinkable ten years ago. It's CRAY! A book about YOU in a
school library! Whatever next?!

Hopefully, as tolerance, understanding and visibility of LGBT*
people increases, homophobia will die out with the ignorant
people it lingers in.

CHAPTER 6:
HATERZ
GON' HATE

Aside from a bit of pesky self-loathing, there are more practical reasons why people might choose not to identify as lesbian, gay, bisexual or trans – or at the very least keep it under their hat. Depending on where you live and the faith you're born into, circumstances can vary wildly. This section, although hardly filled with LOLs, I'm afraid, is really important because, although it's pretty mega being a gay, it's far from comfortable for thousands of people all around the world. And, who knows, we might be able to make a little difference.

What's annoying is that homophobia is a cultural thing. In ancient times, people were super open minded about gay shiz. Look at Sappho on her island; check out the same-sex culture of the Greeks and Romans. I'm afraid the tide turned when Christian missionaries took it upon themselves to travel the world to tell everyone how marriage should be done. From there it was downhill all the way as far as the acceptance of homosexuality was concerned.

If you are reading this book in the UK (or pretty much anywhere in Europe or most of the United States), you should feel very lucky indeed because while bitchy haterz be throwing shade, at least you have the law on your side. As discussed, in the UK you are actively protected.

HISTORY LESSON

Although it seems unthinkable now, it was illegal to be gay in England and Wales until 1967, and Scotland didn't wise up until 1981 (what were they thinking?). Northern Ireland dithered about until 1982. Before these dates, homosexual behaviour between men was considered a crime ('gross indecency') or a mental illness. In 1954, there were some one thousand men in PRISON for being gay.

That lesbian behaviour was never illegal is down to the assumption that two women could not commit 'sodomy', at least in the UK.

Let's talk about ALAN TURING, a guy you really ought to be taught about in school. Basically, this total dude of a code-breaking genius won us the Second World War but was arrested in 1952 for being gay (again, 'gross indecency'). He accepted CHEMICAL CASTRATION as an alternative to a jail sentence, before killing himself in 1954. Not cool.

A major step forward in equality was the change made to the age of consent. After much, MUCH ridiculousness, in which many politicians showed themselves to be flaming ignoramuses or plain homophobes, the age of consent for same-sex men (again men, as there had never been any rules in place for women) was lowered from twenty-one to eighteen and, FINALLY, in 2001, to sixteen. This meant the law recognised that you can't have one set of rules for straight people and another set for those who aren't.

With the equally baffling and frustrating fight for equal marriage now wrapping up at long last, the overt discrimination (as that is precisely what it is) is finally drawing to a close in the UK – but more on marriage later.

Basically, my friends, sometimes being LGBT* in the UK is a bit pants but, as you're about to learn, it could be far, FAR worse . . .

AROUND THE WORLD IN (ALMOST) EIGHTY GAYS

We didn't choose where we were born. We just popped out where our mother happened to be nine months after we were conceived. Similarly, we didn't choose to be gay or bi – our same-sex attraction has been there for as long as we can remember. Likewise, trans people, more often than not, have always felt they weren't in the correct body or at least felt an unease with gender norms.

In an ideal world, it wouldn't matter where you were born OR what your sexual orientation is, but this total lottery is having a severe impact on people all over the world. The UK may have wised up over the past fifty years, but other countries are comparatively in the dark ages concerning LGBT* rights.

All aboard for what I call the TOUR OF SHAME – countries and territories where human rights are more like human wrongs (see what I did there?).

COUNTRIES WHERE NEITHER MEN NOR WOMEN CAN HAVE SAME-SEX SEX

Afghanistan, Algeria, Angola, **Antigua and Barbuda, Barbados**, Belize, Benin, Bhutan, Botswana, Burma (Myanmar), Burundi, Cameroon, Comoros, Djibouti, Dominica, Eritrea, Ethiopia, Guinea, India, Iran, Lebanon, Liberia, Libya, Malawi, **Maldives**, Marshall Islands, Mauritania, **Morocco**, Oman, Pakistan, Qatar, Samoa, Saint Vincent and the Grenadines, São Tomé and Principe, Saudi Arabia, Senegal, Solomon Islands, Somalia, South Sudan, Sudan, Togo, Trinidad and Tobago, **Tunisia**, Uganda, **United Arab Emirates**, Western Sahara, Yemen, Zambia and some parts of Nigeria and Zanzibar, which belongs to Tanzania

COUNTRIES WHERE TWO MEN CANNOT HAVE SEX BUT THERE ARE NO RULES REGARDING WOMEN

Bahrain, Bangladesh, Brunei, Cook Islands, Fiji, Gambia, Grenada, Guyana, **Jamaica**, Kenya, Kiribati, Kuwait, Lesotho, **Malaysia**, **Mauritius**, Namibia, Nauru, Nigeria, Niue, **Northern Cyprus**, Palau, Palestine-Gaza, Papua New Guinea, Saint Kitts and Nevis, **Saint Lucia**, **Seychelles**, Sierra Leone, Singapore, **Sri Lanka**, Swaziland, Tanzania, Tokelau, Tonga, Tuvalu, Turkmenistan, Uzbekistan, Zimbabwe and Chechen Republic in Russia

COUNTRIES WHICH FORBID GAY MALE SEX AND SOMETIMES APPLY THIS TO GAY WOMEN

Syria, Ghana

COUNTRIES WHICH HAVE A HIGHER AGE OF CONSENT FOR SAME-SEX COUPLES

Bahamas, **Bermuda**, Chile, Indonesia, Côte d'Ivoire, Madagascar, Niger, Suriname, Vanuatu, a few states in the United States, and Queensland in Australia

COUNTRIES WHICH APPLY THE DEATH PENALTY – YES DEATH – FOR SAME-SEX COUPLES

Afghanistan, Iran, Maldives, Mauritania, Pakistan, Saudi Arabia, Sudan, United Arab Emirates (i.e. **Dubai**), Yemen and some parts of Nigeria and Somalia, and the Chechen Republic in Russia

These tables are accurate as of winter 2013. With any luck, the lists will shrink all the time until there's no need for this roll call of shame.

Countries DO change their stance; for example Mozambique recently decriminalised same-sex activity . . . Woo hoo! Pop and Party Rings for everyone. However, in December 2013, India went BACKWARDS and RE-criminalised same-sex activity. NO PARTY SNACKS FOR YOU, PARTY POOPERS.

However – and it's a big however – just because any remaining countries have legalised same-sex behaviour doesn't mean that it's EASY to get your funky sex dance on without repercussions. In many places, Indonesia being a good example, it is legal to have same-sex sex, but people would face great hardship if they were 'out'.

Furthermore, the vast majority of 'legal' countries still have all kinds of hideously homophobic legislation in place – no same-sex marriage or civil partnership, no adoption laws . . . many fail to provide even the most basic protection beyond, 'It's legal, what more do you want?' Clearly, this isn't good enough, and campaigners still have a long way to go.

It's easy to think of gay-illegal places as being far, far away. Too far away to worry about. Well, how about Russia, where LGBT* groups are being persecuted despite their legal status? What about Greece, where gay men and female prostitutes are facing mandatory HIV testing against their will? These are our neighbours. Scary, scary stuff.

BRYAN'S STORY

'Bryan', 21, lives in Singapore.

The situation in Singapore is very strange. Even
though gay people are becoming more and more visible,
we have no legal rights. We have Pink Dot SG, which
is a bit like Pride and we have 'Arts Venues' which are
places for gay people to meet up. I have never known
anybody to be arrested but it is illegal for two men
to have sex. I personally don't understand it.
Singapore is a beautiful and tolerant place,
so it's hard to understand why we don't have laws
to protect us.

Transgender — Global Situation

The following table names countries with laws and rules
protecting transgender people:

COUNTRIES WHICH ALLOW PEOPLE TO ADOPT A NEW GENDER IDENTITY (IN MOST CASES FOLLOWING GENDER REASSIGNMENT SURGERY)

Argentina, Australia, Azerbaijan, Belgium, Bolivia, Brazil, Canada, China, Chile, Colombia, Croatia, Cuba, Czech Republic, Ecuador, Finland, France, Germany, Georgia, Greece, Guam, Iceland, Italy, Israel, Japan, Latvia, Malta, Mexico, Moldova, Montenegro, Nepal ('third gender'), Netherlands, New Zealand, Norway, Panama, Pakistan ('third gender'), Peru, Poland, Portugal, Puerto Rico, Romania, Russia, Slovenia, South Africa, South Korea, Spain, Sweden, Switzerland, Taiwan, Turkey, Ukraine, United Kingdom, Uruguay and most parts of the United States

The situation for trans people is hugely unclear around the world – most countries have no clear laws covering the issue, which roughly translates as no protection for trans people. The above countries all have laws protecting you. However, as with LGB rights, many countries on the list might SEEM accepting but in reality things may be quite different. For instance many of the countries in the above box insist on sterilization before a new gender identity is granted. Be fair, I did warn you this section wasn't exactly a barrel of laughs.

What can you do to help?

Personally, I don't think it's enough to be cross about the treatment of LGBT* people across the world. We have to do our little bit, right? For one thing, in the box of gay-illegal countries, I've emboldened places which are popular holiday destinations.

- STEP ONE – DON'T GO THERE: Seriously, hit countries where it hurts – tourist dollars. For one thing, you won't be able to pull while you're there, and for another (and more seriously), what if you had to rely on the police or hospitals in a place where you aren't legally recognised as having equal rights?

I think that a lot of LGBT* people think that because somewhere is tourist friendly, it's gay friendly. This simply isn't the case. Instead of Jamaica or Barbados, go to Grand Cayman. See? Easy. Do your homework.

- STEP TWO – SUPPORT CHARITY: We can help the fight by supporting groups doing the fighting for us.

Amnesty International: Challenges governments and authorities to fulfil their responsibility to protect LGBT* people from such abuses. The organisation campaigns to protect human rights defenders who put themselves at risk by speaking out against abuses based on sexuality or gender identity.

The Kaleidoscope Trust: Urges the British government, the Commonwealth, the European Union and others to use their power and influence to support the rights of LGBT* people. The trust works with parliamentarians, government ministers, officials and policy makers to try to effect real change in the lives of LGBT* communities around the world.

ILGA: ILGA's aim is to work for the equality of lesbian, gay, bisexual, trans and intersex people and their liberation from all forms of discrimination. The group seeks to achieve this aim through the worldwide cooperation and mutual support of their members.

Stonewall: Stonewall is renowned for its campaigning and lobbying. Some major successes include helping achieve the equalisation of the age of consent, lifting the ban on lesbians and gay men serving in the military, securing legislation allowing same-sex couples to adopt, and the repeal of Section 28, (which prevented same-sex education in schools). More recently, Stonewall has helped secure civil partnerships and ensured that the Equality Act (2010)

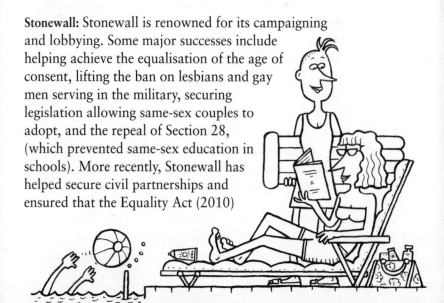

protected lesbians and gay men in terms of goods and services (for example, hotels can't refuse you and your partner a room because you're a same sex couple).

All four of these groups rely on donations. This means you need to jolly well stick your hand in your pocket and donate whatever you can. Some charities are listed in the 'Helpful numbers and websites and stuff' section at the back of this book.

THE GAYS VERSUS RELIGION

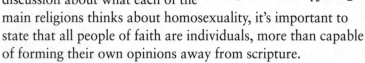

You know when we said it's not very nice when people say that ALL gay men are like this or ALL lesbians are like that? WELL, it's similarly shoddy to claim that ALL Christians think like this or ALL Muslims think like that. Before we get into a discussion about what each of the main religions thinks about homosexuality, it's important to state that all people of faith are individuals, more than capable of forming their own opinions away from scripture.

To be honest, most people of faith probably don't give a flying fig about who you're snogging – they're probably worrying about their gas bill or whether they left their hair straighteners on.

However, although most religious people are somewhat progressive, there are individuals and regimes that insist on clinging to multi-thousand-year-old bits of paper in the name of hate. If you look back at the list of gay-illegal countries, they do tend to be the ones where the legal system is tied to a religious regime – not naming names but, like, you know, Saudi Arabia.

Before I tear some old religious stuff to shreds, **I have faith that the vast, vast majority of religious people use (whichever) God's teaching to find tolerance and love for all mankind. And also womankind** (yeah, some religions are mega sexist too).

Most people of religion see their sacred texts as a general guide for life – moral guidance, as it were. The problem comes when a minority take the written words literally – and the meaning of some of these words may even have been misinterpreted. Sacred stories and poems were written down by humans hundreds of years ago and so may have errors or mistranslations or additions. It's sort of like playing a game of Chinese whispers that's lasted for centuries – some things are bound to get lost along the way.

The closest thing I personally have to a prophet is Madonna. Now what if I went around taking everything she said literally?

Look at the lyrics to 'Express Yourself' and 'Material Girl'. . . contradictory at best, I'm sure you'll agree!

Let's take a look at the main world religions and examine their traditional views first on homosexuality, then transgenderism.

1. Hinduism and Buddhism

Let's start with the positive. Hinduism and Buddhism are way chilled out about both homosexuality and trans issues. Hindu art depicts various figures engaging in same-sex acts, while the whole point of Buddhism is about being at one with the world, which, in this case, includes us.

Hurrah for Hinduism and Buddhism!

2. Christianity

As you know, there are various branches of the Christian church, and they each take a different stance on homosexuality. Here's a best-fit guide:

- **Church of England:** Progressive, but resistant. Same-sex marriage is OK for normal folks but not priests.

- **Catholic Church:** Homosexuality is considered a sin.

- **Methodist Church:** Pretty cool comparatively.

- **Quakers:** Mad cool. They've been cool for years.

- **Baptists:** They have a huge problem with the gays, I'm afraid.

So what's the big problem? Well, it's all about TRANSLATION and LANGUAGE. There are lots of translations of the Bible (the Christian holy book), and all of them are slightly different. The odd word here and there looks pretty bad for homosexuality. The issues stem from two key parts of the Bible. The quotes below are from the King James Bible, and I've put them in a SCARY FONT. No reason . . .

'AND THEY CALLED UNTO LOT, AND SAID UNTO HIM, WHERE ARE THE MEN WHICH CAME IN TO THEE THIS NIGHT? BRING THEM OUT UNTO US, THAT WE MAY KNOW THEM.' Genesis 19:5 (In this instance, 'to know' is thought to mean 'to bum'.)

'EVEN AS SODOM AND GOMORRAH, AND THE CITIES ABOUT THEM IN LIKE MANNER, GIVING THEMSELVES OVER TO FORNICATION, AND GOING AFTER STRANGE FLESH, ARE SET FORTH FOR AN EXAMPLE, SUFFERING THE VENGEANCE OF ETERNAL FIRE.' Jude 1:7 ('Strange flesh' is thought to mean, in this case, 'bum'.)

So what's goin' on here? In a nutshell, the towns of Sodom and Gomorrah used to be in the Jordan valley until divine judgement was passed and they were destroyed by heavenly fire. Sounds like an awesome episode of Buffy until you realise that people use this story to persecute people.

In some interpretations of the Hebrew text (versions of this story appear in the Torah, Bible and Quran) it's thought the behaviour that displeased God so much was homosexuality.

This is WIDELY open to interpretation as we shall soon discover.

More eye-roll inducing admonition from the book of Leviticus:

'THOU SHALT NOT LIE WITH MANKIND, AS WITH WOMANKIND: IT IS ABOMINATION.' **Leviticus 18:22**

'IF A MAN ALSO LIE WITH MANKIND, AS HE LIETH WITH A WOMAN, BOTH OF THEM HAVE COMMITTED AN ABOMINATION: THEY SHALL SURELY BE PUT TO DEATH; THEIR BLOOD SHALL BE UPON THEM.' Leviticus 20:13

Way harsh.

HOW TO ARGUE WITH A CHRISTIAN

So if you have the misfortune to stumble onto a literalist, homophobic Christian, how do you go about defending yourself? Knowledge is power, my friend.

IF THEY COME AT YOU WITH 'IT'S IN THE BIBLE!'

Let's talk about translation. The Bible has been translated and interpreted many, many times. We can't be one hundred per cent certain what the original even said, so it's insane to take it literally. This is true of any translated or interpreted text. Even the various modern versions of the Bible are different, so how can one possibly take it all literally?

Point out that the text was written thousands of years ago. Times have changed. The messages are still somewhat applicable, but we have to adapt them for modern living. Also point out that ALL of the above extracts are out of context, and at the end of the day, they are stories, not laws (even the Apostle Paul decreed this).

Contexts change. The Bible repeatedly refers to going after taxmen – who at the time were crooked. You don't hear about Christians chasing after HMRC with flaming torches, do you?

Also, lady lovers, as the problem all stems from 'sodomy', lesbians are automatically off the hook anyway! Whoop!

Finally, in the New Testament, based on the teachings of Jesus, Jesus said precisely NOTHING on the subject. As we know, Jesus taught nothing but love and tolerance. Personally, I think Jesus, had he lived today, would be on every Pride march.

HOW TO ARGUE WITH SODOM AND GOMORRAH

Firstly, the phrase 'to know' (from the Hebrew) very rarely means 'to bum'. In this case, it most likely means 'interrogate'. Secondly, it is thought the 'strange flesh' refers to that of the angels or possibly bestiality. In either case, most Biblical scholars agree that the towns were struck down primarily for their greed and uncharitable nature. There is no CLEAR reference to homosexuality.

HOW TO ARGUE WITH LEVITICUS

OK, I grant you this one is a little more clear cut, BUT – there's a big BUT (tee-hee). Basically, Leviticus is meant to be a list of instructions from Moses to the Levites and, yes, the one above was one of the rules. But, luckily for us, the rest of the list was CRAY. So anyone throwing a bit of Leviticus your way should also be prepared to

Sell their daughter into slavery.

Never make any physical contact with a woman on her period.

Burn bulls.

Never eat shellfish (also an abomination, so BEWARE THE PRAWN)

Never trim the hair around their head. This is forbidden.

So, as you can see, you'd have to be a pretty massive hypocrite to use this one as an argument against homosexuality.

Here's a twist you might not have seen coming:

There's some fairly convincing evidence of gay love IN THE BIBLE almost three thousand years prior to Queer as Folk. That's right. In the book of Second Samuel, besties David and Jonathan may have been a little more than friends! Check it out:

'I AM DISTRESSED FOR THEE, MY BROTHER JONATHAN: VERY PLEASANT HAS THOU BEEN UNTO ME: THY LOVE TO ME WAS WONDERFUL, PASSING THE LOVE OF WOMEN.' 2 Samuel 1:26 (You go gurlz!)

And the gals were getting on board the sexy Bible love train too. The story of Ruth and Naomi reads like an episode of *Desperate Housewives* on crack – there's a LOT of husband swapping – but some scholars read their journey as same-sex love.

Finally, there are various bits of the Bible that are conveniently missing – see the Gospel of Mary – so, as ever, we mustn't wholly trust such ancient sources of information.

3. Islam

A little like the Bible, there's not an awful lot in the Quran to explicitly forbid homosexual behaviour, although it also refers to the people of Sodom and Gomorrah, this time with a more explicit focus on rape, not homosexuality. Well, we already know how to respond to that story, don't we.

The larger problem comes from the Hadith, or teachings
of Muhammad. These are . . . erm . . . less ambiguous.

'WHOEVER YOU FIND COMMITTING THE SIN OF THE PEOPLE OF
LUT (LOT), KILL THEM, BOTH THE ONE WHO DOES IT AND THE
ONE TO WHOM IT IS DONE.'
Sunan al-Tirmidhi.

Well, at least it doesn't discriminate between the bottom
and top.

HOW TO ARGUE WITH MUSLIMS

The good news is that the Quran is on your side. NOWHERE in
there does Allah state a punishment for homosexual behaviour.
What's more, the Quran actively encourages diversity, as Allah
created that too:

'O MANKIND! WE CREATED YOU FROM A SINGLE (PAIR) OF A
MALE AND A FEMALE AND MADE YOU INTO NATIONS AND
TRIBES THAT YE MAY KNOW EACH OTHER (NOT THAT YE MAY
DESPISE EACH OTHER). VERILY THE MOST HONOURED OF YOU
IN THE SIGHT OF ALLAH IS (HE WHO IS) THE MOST RIGHTEOUS
OF YOU. AND ALLAH HAS FULL KNOWLEDGE AND IS WELL
ACQUAINTED (WITH ALL THINGS).' Yusuf Ali Quran 49:13

Regarding the Hadith, as with Leviticus, there are various rules
that very few people would follow today – seduction by women
is on a par with homosexual acts, so it would seem, as is

drinking wine. I'm sure we wouldn't kill people for these things. Moreover, the sharia law sets no specific punishment for homosexual behaviour – recommending the death penalty only be used for adultery, renouncing the faith and murder. Most Muslim countries don't enforce these punishments (side eye at those who do).

4. Judaism

Not being funny, but these guys kinda started it. The parts of the Bible that deal with homosexuality came from the bits based on the Torah (the Pentateuch), so it's pretty much the same story – the general negative feeling towards homosexuality comes from Sodom and Gomorrah and Leviticus, in this case called Vayiqra.

As with Christianity, there are many branches of the Jewish faith and, unsurprisingly, the Orthodox branch tends to be the most, well, orthodox. One of the most popular forms of Judaism, **Reform Judaism**, is way more chilled and doesn't prohibit gay, lesbian or bisexual couples from entering the faith. So let's all send them a cookie.

* * *

LUKE'S STORY

Apparently as a boy of around 4 or 5 years old there was an occasion in which I came home in tears from school - someone had told me that God didn't exist.

As a child I was also known for my re-enactments of
Disney films and performing Cher's 'Shoop Shoop Song'
for anyone that would sit around long enough to
endure it; this led my parents to believe that I'd
either be a Vicar or an actor (why actor and not Drag
Queen I'm not sure, I'm told I played the part of
Cinderella wonderfully). It turns out that I'm neither
Vicar nor actor (nor Drag Queen, although I do have
the legs for it) but I still retain that same faith I
had 20-odd years ago.

I grew up not in a traditionally Christian family but
we began to attend Church when we moved to Sussex
shortly before my 9th Birthday and it soon became a
very important part of my life and my development.
Much of my free time as a teenager was spent
volunteering with the children's and youth work at
our local Baptist Church and I had a close group of
friends who would do the same. The painful irony was
that they only knew just one aspect of me, no matter
how much time we spent in each other's company.

Growing up and from a young age knowing that you're
gay (I asked out my first "boyfriend" aged 10) yet
being reminded fairly consistently that "God's best is
man and woman" is a damaging place to be. It causes
many people to lose their faith, many to self-harm
and many to take their lives. It's a hurtful place
that countless young people and adults' alike still
find themselves in today and the Church has a lot of
work to do to make amends there.

However, this being said I consider myself to be in an incredibly privileged position now that I've come through those imposed dark places. I came to own my faith personally and not have it prescribed to me by dogmatic teaching; my Theological studies aided this journey and allowed me to realise I belong to two beautiful, charismatic, joyful and alive communities that in spite of their differences often look at life in just the same way.

Being a Christian who also happens to be gay, or being a gay man who also happens to have a faith, is often a troublesome path to tread, neither community really quite understanding how you can belong to both fully but I find it to be an incredibly energising adventure to be part of.

As a Christian I believe that God is love and where there is love God is there; one of the most loving communities I know belongs to "the gays" and so this is where I know God dwells.

- Luke

RELIGION AND TRANSGENDERISM

This one throws up more problems. Before we start, it's worth noting that gender reassignment, as we know it today, wasn't possible when the key holy texts were being written. Therefore there really isn't a precedent for it. There are, however, a few passages on cross-dressing which have been skewed to encapsulate all gender dysphoria.

Paradoxically, Islam takes a fairly chilled view on this. There's nothing specific in the Quran, and the Hadith takes issue only where 'cross-dressing' is used for prostitution (which isn't a brilliant career option, let's be honest, so they probably have a point). However, in some countries, gender reassignment surgery (often male to female) is seen as a 'cure' for homosexuality, which is a crime. This clearly isn't ideal.

Christianity and Judaism have more defined and, indeed, negative views about gender reassignment. In Deuteronomy of the Old Testament (and similarly in the Torah), there appears the following passage:

'A WOMAN MUST NOT WEAR MEN'S CLOTHING NOR A MAN WEAR WOMEN'S FOR THE LORD GOD DETESTS ANYONE WHO DOES THIS.'
Deuteronomy 22:5

There are also references to eunuchs (men with their sexual organs removed) not being able to enter the temple.

As with the passages that address homosexuality, trans people are more than able to defend themselves should the Bible or

Jewish scripture be used to attack them. In the case of Deuteronomy, the text appears to refer to cross-dressing, not gender dysmorphia and, given the era it was written in, could actually be about practices of pagan fertility cults at the time. Furthermore, the eunuchs back then weren't castrated to change gender; many were slaves who had their bits chopped off against their will. Once more we can see that many of the rules applicable to the people of biblical times simply aren't relevant any more.

Finally, in the book of John, the author talks about Jesus's inclusive view of those born with birth defects, and I think we can argue being born the wrong gender is indeed one such defect. I love it when you can actually use the Bible to argue in our favour.

Furthermore, the concept of third gender stems from Hindu teaching and philosophy. This category encompasses all genders that exist outside of simply male and female and is often legally recognised. In some cultures and rituals, members of the third gender are revered as having almost magical powers and are considered lucky. So, see, it's not all bad, is it?

A Final Note:

A dear friend once told me, 'YOU CAN'T ARGUE WITH CRAZY.' Someone else once said, 'HATERZ GON' HATE.' Put these two pieces of wisdom together and you kind of have the situation we're in. People using religion to hate LGBT* people are going to do so however well we argue our case. You'll spout logic until you're blue in the face and some homophobes will continue to hate.

I believe if you wanted to piece together a convincing argument about why steak and kidney pie was sinful, you would be able to use religious texts to help your campaign – they are old enough and vague enough to damn almost anything.

All we can do is rest assured that we are far from an abomination. Whether you believe in God as a creator or not, we were all born out of something very natural. We are one hundred per cent organic. Like orange juice with bits.

CHAPTER 7:
COMING OUT

Resisting reruns of *SpongeBob SquarePants* while revising; avoiding the shark-like gaze of your cruel, capricious maths teacher; trying to think of something hilarious-but-alluring to say to that person you're dying to snog – your school years are pretty tough. As if all that wasn't hard enough, the average age at which people usually 'come out' as gay, lesbian or bi is now seventeen years old – while still at school or college. Just one more thing to worry about, and it's not on the curriculum.

How to do it? When to do it? Whom to tell? To tell at all? Coming out is a potential minefield. One wrong step and your metaphorical gay leg will be blown clean off.

Seriously, though. For a young LGBT* person, there is NOTHING more terrifying than the idea of telling your nearest and dearest that you fancy people with the same bits as you or that you've pretty much had enough of your original gender. This fear is perfectly reasonable, but there are ways in which we can make the transition from 'closet case' to 'out and proud' as smooth as caramel.

What is 'coming out'?

In the olden days (and to this very day in some rather traditional quarters), fancy young society women, known as debutantes, were dressed up and paraded around for potential suitors and the like. These events were known as 'coming out parties', and this is where we get the term 'coming out'. Before the First World War, the phrase meant more to 'come out' into society.

These days, we refer in particular to 'coming out of the closet', an American slang term for no longer concealing one's identity. Once you're ready to let the world know about your identity, you are no longer 'closeted' or 'on the down-low'.

The word 'identity' is key. 'Coming out' isn't when you first swap love juice with someone of your own gender, but rather the public adoption of a label. It's telling people.

As I've said numerous times, labels aren't for everyone. Lots of people may choose to have sexyfuntimes with people of the same gender without identifying as gay or lesbian, just as a gay man who has sex with a woman isn't automatically straight. ('Hallelu! He's seen the light!' Yeah, that's not gonna happen). The process of establishing an identity can take years. The good news is, no one is stuck with one label for their whole life. Many people change their sexual identity as they become more comfortable with themselves and their sex lives.

The same is true of gender labels. Gender doesn't have to be concrete.

One only has to look at the thriving queer club scene to see hot young things experimenting with traditional gender roles. These have nothing to do with sexuality, as we've discussed.

At its core, 'coming out' is the part where you tell someone what your sexual or gender orientation is – and that can be anything.

Why 'come out' at all?

Perhaps the real question is: is there any benefit to coming out? The answer is almost certainly . . .

YES!

People cheerfully profess their religion, marital status, ethnic origin and favourite food, but discussion of sexual orientation or gender remains uniquely taboo. Perhaps with good reason.

As we have learned, there are eighty countries where men and women can be prosecuted for having sex with someone of the same gender. MEGA POLITICAL SADFACE.

If it is safe to 'come out', however, there are many benefits to doing so. At the end of the day, desires, crushes, dating and relationships are a massive part of anyone's life, and hiding something so vital from your friends and family is both hard work and isolating. It may sound trite, but 'being yourself' is good for you. Sharing is caring, yo!

'For me, the main benefit was a general sense of ease
- I no longer had to hide where I was going, why I had

the letters "G-A-Y" stamped on my wrist or the
uncomfortable feelings when asked why I didn't have
a boyfriend or what kind of boys I liked.'

Mica, 23, London.

The single phrase mentioned time after time after time in the survey was 'a weight off my shoulders'. So cliché, but so, so true.

On a more practical level, once a young person has 'come out' as gay, lesbian, bisexual or trans, it is that much easier to find like-minded people. Allsorts Youth Project, just one example of an LGBT* group for young people in Brighton, has a weekly club night where young people can socialise in a safe space – without the need for gay bars or clubs. (More on that in chapter 8.)

Furthermore, once a person chooses to identify as gay, lesbian, bisexual or trans, you'd be surprised at how supportive family and friends can be. Very often, parents and friends have already worked it out, and 'coming out' leads to a closer, more honest relationship with the people you love the most. Perhaps best of all, they'll stop trying to fix you up with people who are the wrong sex!

Finally, don't underestimate the personal satisfaction and pride you'll feel at simply being yourself. It's freeing.

'There are so many [advantages to coming out] that it's
hard to know where to start. The main things are to
know that you will still be loved, and that you are
happy and contented in who you really are. I was so

worried about how my family would react to my
sexuality that it used to keep me awake at night . . .
now I know how well [coming out to them] went, I wish
that I had talked to them sooner. It took a few months
to adjust to being open about my sexuality, but it
definitely made me closer to my family. I did run into
some issues with bullying at school, being the first
boy to "come out". Once I was accepted (begrudgingly) as
a part of the school, I think it was easier for others
to be honest. I was very lucky in that I had some good
teachers, lots of friends and my family for support.'

Mike, UK.

Why 'stay in'?

Of course, there may be good reasons why people choose not to
discuss their sexual or gender identity. For one, it does often
seem that there are three choices – straight, gay or bi. Sometimes
it's just not that simple, so defining yourself may take more time.

Moreover, some communities and religions believe that
homosexuality is wrong. That doesn't prevent anyone from being
lesbian, gay or bisexual but rather restricts their ability to be
'out', as this may mean they feel their parents and friends might
not be supportive of them.

The worry of what family and friends might think or do is what
keeps people in 'the closet' more than any other factor, regardless
of background. Remember, every 'out' gay or bisexual man or
woman and every 'out' trans person has gone through this

process and survived the ordeal. Most retain the family and friends they had before they 'came out'.

When it goes wrong

The fear that you'll be disowned, shamed and tossed out onto the street is absolutely the worst-case scenario and one that very rarely happens. There may be friends who are unable to accept your new identity, and that's sad, but you can always make new friends. The worst fear is that your family, especially your parents, might react badly. At first many do – I won't lie – but with time, nearly all build a bridge and get over it.

If (and I can't stress how rare this is) the situation becomes so bad that you have to leave home, there is support out there. Some people live with other family members or family friends. Alternatively, Young People's services will be able to refer you to the right people who can help you. There's a list of groups near you at the back of the book.

'It started when my mum saw me hugging a friend on Facebook. She is Catholic - very Catholic - and for months I was getting, "You're gay - I'm gonna kick you out". After about two months of this, something in my head snapped and I said, "I'm not gay, I don't know what I am!" I was fourteen. Two days later I got kicked out. I had to work ... I worked in a Chinese takeaway. Eventually I became a chef, and now I own my home.'

Shane, 23, Shoreham-By-Sea.

'I'm Coming Out. I want the world to know.'

So you've decided you might identify as LGBT*? The hardest part – admitting it to yourself – is done. But how to tell everyone else?

I decided it was time to come out about six months after my Dean Cain–based revelation. I told a very close friend whom I trusted not to write it on the sixth-form common room noticeboard. She had also done a very good job of signalling to me that she was A-OK with THE GAYS. As a young questioning person, you would do well to surround yourself with cool, open-minded people – it lubes the passage out of the closet, as it were.

I chose to tell her – well, 'chose' isn't the right word; rather it popped out as I carried a treacle tart home from school one day. (I stress I had made the tart earlier in a home economics class. I don't just carry cakes around to make people like me.)

Predictably, my friend was cool and reassuring and herself came out as queer in the same conversation, so I felt a million times better. To this day, though, I cannot eat treacle tart without feeling like my world might come crashing in around me, as it did that night after I had come out – because even though my afternoon had been perfectly pleasant, the cat was now out of the bag, and I couldn't get the furry bugger back in it. That is always going to be scary.

I adjusted quickly. Over the following weeks, I talked about boys CONSTANTLY, making up for lost time, and within a few weeks I was happily telling my friend and a couple of other friends which boy I'd most like to snog on the rugby team. It was all fine and I haven't looked back.

I came out to my parents much later – I waited until I was living away from home and able to support myself financially. You can decide if that was cowardly or sensible. In the end, my mum actually asked me outright and I answered her honestly. I got my stepmum to tell my dad!

Every LGBT* person's experiences are different, but here are the dos and don'ts of coming out:

DO

DON'T

DO	DON'T
Tell someone you trust, someone you feel comfortable talking with and who you think won't tell the whole world until you're ready.	Leave your Internet browser full of, erm, 'specialist' movies. You'd be shocked how many people are outed this way.
Put feelers out as to your family's or friend's attitudes to LGBT* people before discussing it with them. Listen to what they're saying about other gay people to get an idea of whether they're a 'safe' person to tell.	Forget the professionals – teachers and GPs are trained to listen to exactly these sorts of issues, and they may offer valuable advice. You might even get a jazzy pamphlet.
Talk to people who've been through it all before – other LGBT* people. See how they survived!	Be dramatic. Your sister's wedding is NOT the best time to leap into the aisle, block the bride's path and scream: 'I LOVE COCK.'
Pick your moment – find a quiet, safe space.	Do it by email or text – the written word is easy to misinterpret. ('You're coming out where honey? Will you still be home in time for dinner?' etc)
Celebrate. Once you've done it, it can feel like you've opened Pandora's box, but the hardest part is done.	Come out because someone else, even a partner, says you should. You have to do it when YOU'RE ready.
Read this book ;-)	Come out just because you have a boyfriend or girlfriend – those you tell are much more likely to think it's a 'phase' that will last as long as the relationship.

Don't just take it from me

Every 'out' gay or bisexual or trans man or woman has been through it all before!

'I first told my then boyfriend. We'd only been going out about a fortnight, and he came out as transvestite to me as we were curled up in bed together, so it only seemed right that I told him I was bi.'

Sarah, 35, Ireland.

'I told my friend in the tiny music practice room in our school. It amuses me today to think that most people come OUT of the closet. I came out IN a closet. I thought I was bisexual at first, although, in retrospect, I think that I was having difficulty understanding the difference between the strong kinship I felt with my female friends and the sexual attraction I had to other boys. It felt like a large part of puberty was finding out the answer to this conundrum.'

Rick, 29, UK.

'[I came out on a] residential trip to France. My gay friend asked me how I felt about her being gay, and I said I was OK. She asked me if I was straight. I said no. We carried on talking about how sh•t the French weather was when you had to do an assault course in the mud.'

Nina, 16, UK.

'[I first told] People at my halls of residence at uni. We went on a night out just before Christmas, and I made sure they were all there and told them one by one. The first was someone I had gotten really close to, and after that, admittedly with a drink or two inside me, it got easier.'

Chris, Manchester.

'I first told a girl I was friends with at school. I was sixteen and we were at a party, and we went for a long walk and had a deep and meaningful. She told me she was in love with another one of our friends, and I said I really fancied our art teacher.'

L, 28, Brighton.

Of course . . . it's not always so smooth. Coming out can be tough.

'I told my girlfriend at the time, whom I'd been with for three years, about my thoughts and feelings regarding my desire to transition to female, my self-view as female and my experimentation over the past number of years. She broke up with me then and there, refusing to discuss it.'

Laura, 21, UK.

'The first person I told was a female friend who believed she was in love with me. She was married and had made it clear that she was prepared to abandon that to be with me. I felt like I owed it to her to explain why that could never happen.'

BFL, 43, Minnesota, USA.

'My stepmum discovered photos from the Internet that I had printed at college . . . It kind of went from there!'

Dani, 29, Newcastle upon Tyne.

A handy script

Friends are relatively easy to come out to, as you've (presumably) picked mates who aren't total douches. Some LGBT* people are in heterosexual or cisgender relationships when they figure it out, and it can be very hard to tell a partner that you're not (exclusively) sexually interested in them.

But most LGBT* people worry the most about telling their parents. It really scares the plop out of us. Why? Well, they knew us as babies, and coming out (as gay, bi or lesbian) is essentially offering a delightful insight into your sexual desires.

Something NO ONE enjoys saying: 'Hey, Mum, you'll never guess what I like having up my bum!' See my point?

For trans people, some parents see it as a bit of a slap in the face. Like they GAVE you your assigned gender and they RAISED you accordingly. As with sexuality, though, it often comes as no surprise, and many parents can be hugely supportive of transgender children – even very young ones. There are support groups, such as MERMAIDS, for parents of trans children (see 'Helpful numbers and websites and stuff' at the back of the book).

Coming out is as personal as your identity. The following is only a guide – a one-size-fits all approach for you to adapt.

1. Pick your time

It might be spontaneous, or you might plan a specific time (although the build-up would be TORTURE). A lot of LGBT* people seem to use the TV as a prompt; i.e. bringing it up when gay rights are mentioned in the news or when gay couples are shown in soaps (which is pretty much every day). Whatever time you pick, I think a 1-2-1 conversation is always best.

2. Pick a venue

Remember, your loved ones might need a bit of time to process, so I wouldn't recommend a Topshop changing room. Nine times out of ten, home is best, or at the very least an establishment that serves tea. Tea makes everything OK – remember that. (Do you have somewhere to go if they need some space – could you pop round to a mate's house?)

3. Is it safe?

Your safety is more important than anything else on earth. Do you live in Saudi Arabia or one of the eighty-ish countries (see chapter 6) where you might be locked up or stoned to death? Look into getting a passport.

Joking aside, if your parents have expressed homophobic sentiments in the past, it may be wise to make a plan B should they react badly. A lot of people choose to wait until they have a degree of independence before taking this step. Make contact with gay youth groups – a list of which are at the back of this book – and ensure you have support should things go awry.

OK, so now we've set it all up, here are some openers:

'I really wanted to talk to you about something . . .'

Now, at this stage, it's possible your parent(s) might say, 'Is this about your being gay?' VERY OFTEN parents have got an inkling. This is exactly how my mum dragged me out of the closet.

If they don't, however . . .

'For a while now, I've been attracted to men/women/men AND women' or 'I identify much more as a guy than I do a girl' (or vice versa).

Then . . .

'Nothing's changed. I'm still exactly the same person you know, and I hated keeping that a secret from you.'

And then give them a chance to reply. You might be surprised and delighted.

'I told my parents I was bisexual at twenty. They were conservatively religious, but they told me they loved me just the same. I told them I was actually gay shortly after turning twenty-two, and this time they didn't bat an eyelid.'

Stephen, 22, Johannesburg, South Africa.

'I told them both, although separately, as they are divorced, and each one was in a pub while we were having dinner. They were a little taken aback, but after a while, I think after they had thought about it for a bit, they realised that it explained a lot of my previous behaviour and appearance. They couldn't care less now and are happy that I am happy.'

Jools, 38, Madrid, Spain.

But what if they're not happy? Some likely objections:

LIKELY OBJECTION	RESPONSE
Are you sure?	I really am. I've felt this way for a very long time. It's just that now I'm comfortable talking about it with you.
Is it a phase?	No. (See above.)
You're not gay*! (*or lesbian, bi, trans etc)	I am. I know this must be a bit of a shock, but I've always been this way. It just took me this long to figure it out.
Could you try not being . . . ?	No. I've given this a lot of thought. I'm telling you because I need to be honest about who I am.
I don't believe it!	I've had loads of time to think about this. I understand you'll need some time to process what I'm telling you.
Don't tell anyone else!	I can't promise that. I can give you some time to think about what I've said, but I need to be honest about who I am.

Keep strong and listen to Lady Gaga's *Born this Way*. Or simply present them with this very book and get them to turn to this chapter!

After you've told them, back off. You're not going to pester anyone into being fine. You've probably known for much longer than they have. Also try to remember that the reason a lot of parents flip their weaves on finding out is that they're CONCERNED out of LOVE. Remember how I said that coming out is accepting a place in a persecuted minority. The fact of the matter is, identifying as LGBT* is going to make your life that little bit harder . . . and no parent actively wants that for their kids.

Accept that they need their own time to accept your new identity. It may take minutes, days, months or even years. They will come around in time. They stand to lose something hugely valuable if they don't: YOU. Remember, there are groups out there especially for LGBT* youths. Should things go wrong, there is help out there (see 'Building a Bridge' at the back of the book).

'I promised myself I would tell my parents if I ever had a boyfriend (I felt that being in a relationship and having to hide it was possibly the crappiest thing ever) - and so I did. I came out during the Easter holidays just after having been asked out by this boy. My parents were surprised and shocked - they hadn't suspected a thing - and it was weird talking about my gay feelings with them to start with, but over the past year we've all gotten more comfortable about it.'

R, 17, London.

If you're ready to come out, congratulations! Now you've got your membership card, you're joining a legacy of people who've gone before, a sense of belonging and queer culture – should you want it. The most important thing is that you are now free to be you AND shout about it from the rooftops. Or not – it's your choice.

Coming Out as Trans

Coming out as LGB* is relatively easy compared with coming out as trans. Once you've come out, life pretty much carries on as normal. WHAT? THERE ISN'T A PARADE DOWN THE HIGH STREET? No, I'm afraid not.

Becoming trans requires work. Situations vary wildly. Some young trans people have been dressing in clothes often assigned to the opposite gender* since they were little kids. Some people have been doing so in secret or in a performance-based way as a drag queen or king.

*You'll note that a lot of this crap wouldn't be necessary if society didn't have such closed ideas of what a man should dress like and what a woman should dress like.

When a person comes out as trans, it could mean admitting they sometimes like to cross-dress or that they intend to identify as their chosen gender full-time. As with sexuality, it's the admitting it aloud part that's terrifying. This time, however, people expect a physical transformation afterwards.

The process is unique to every individual, but for people wishing to **transition** into a new gender full-time, there is a set plan. For most people, the first port of call is their GP. People under the age of eighteen will be referred to the Child and Adolescent Mental Health Services (CAMHS), while adults will be referred to a specialist gender dysphoria clinic or a psychiatrist. That is not to say that being trans is a mental illness of itself, but when dealing with such a big step it's important to establish it's the correct choice.

The NHS now recommends swift action for people desiring to transition. There are guidelines on the NHS website that you can take along to your GP, as most won't be experts on this. Once you've been referred, you may well start on hormone treatment – for MTF patients, this involves taking oestrogen, and for FTM, testosterone. The effects are sudden and, in some cases, irreversible.

It is important to seek medical help instead of self-administering hormones. The results are better. End of.

Hormones will change how you look and sound, but some trans people also opt for surgery. Some surgical procedures are available on the NHS, but some would have to be bought privately (like facial feminisation procedures). To have genital surgery (it's worth pointing out here that a huge percentage of

FTM transsexuals never have a phalloplasty – or winky job),
most surgeons require you to have been living in your chosen
gender for about two years.

Obviously, genital surgery is painful and the recovery period is
lengthy, so some people choose to not have it. Others, however,
feel they need a full physical overhaul. It's very much about
choice and understanding what's right for you.

One thing is for certain: if you or someone you know comes out
as trans, the most important element is the new identity.
Choosing a name and making sure everyone uses the **correct
pronouns** is as important as how you dress and look.

IRENE'S STORY

Irene, 33, is an MTF transsexual from New Jersey, USA.

I opted for hormones, after taking some time to be
sure I wanted this, because it had been my
understanding that they are a very important medical
step that can produce profound changes in body and
mind. For some people, they're more important even
than the things that we have to do through surgery,
but I wouldn't go that far for myself.

I'm given to understand that I personally am on the
slower end of the scale of how fast changes tend to
occur. I've been on hormone therapy for eighteen
months now. It was quite exciting for the first couple

months, and still is every time I notice some new
progress. For a while, I would measure my chest with a
tape measure to reassure myself that things were
happening there. It wasn't frightening at all; this
has always been my fondest desire, and it's a quite
gentle process, really; there's nothing to be scared by.

As far as what changed, the first thing I noticed was
that my nipples became developed - that is, stopped
being shrivelled up like male ones are. Then, over
about three months, my hips widened, from thirty-two
inches to forty inches! I was still presenting as male
at work during that period, so that was a little
difficult for me, since I couldn't wear my actual
wardrobe and had to find male slacks that sort of fit.

Something should probably be said about facial-hair
removal, by the way. Hormones don't do that (nor do
they change the voice, which has to be done through
practice and often special training), so I had
sessions for that every weekend. There's a controversy
about whether laser treatment or electrolysis is
better, which prevents there being good advice in the
community on it. The facts are that laser covers many
times more follicles per session, while electrolysis
is always permanent, even on tough follicles. So what
everybody winds up doing is laser to get a clear face
at first and electrolysis later on to finish the job.

But nobody gave me this advice! So I just went for
electrolysis, concurrently with starting hormones,

because I didn't know any better. It was intensely painful, but I actually viewed that as a good thing, since it gave me some concrete sense of progress that I wasn't getting from the hormones at that time. Also, since most trans women (though I hardly knew any back then) have been through it at some point, there was a sense of belonging, which was nice.

For the first eight months or so, I had virtually no breast growth - enough that I could tell things had happened, with my shirt off, but it was quite distressing. They finally did start growing - I talked to my doctor and we played with my dosages a little - but I've never had the 'growing pains' sensation that almost everybody mentions. As of today, I wear a B cup, but I don't really fill it.

I don't view that hormone therapy, nor the genital surgery that I am also seeking, as cosmetic at all; it's correcting a vital mismatch between body and soul. But the insurance company will see it that way on both counts (what could be less cosmetic than a complete change of genitalia?), so I'll be paying out of pocket.

I've spoken with other trans women on the subject, and most agree that there is an improved capacity to feel emotion. I can definitely confirm that in my own experience; it's too pronounced to be psychosomatic. Frankly, I don't like the person who I was before starting hormones, and I never want to be that cold-hearted again. Also, I am able to summon tears when I feel the need, nowadays, which I never was before. Tears are very liberating.

In addition to increased emotionality, I had an almost immediate mood improvement. I had been depressed my whole life. For probably ten years prior to hormones, I was also deeply suicidal, making two very serious attempts - with subsequent hospitalizations. Once I got some oestrogen in my system, I could no longer notice depressive 'spiral' thinking patterns in myself. Even my psychiatrist saw a profound difference and ultimately took me off most of the psychiatric medications she had had me on, because, as we both agreed, they were no longer relevant to me. It was a complete turnaround, which is something that 'just depression' patients never, ever experience. Beyond doubt, oestrogen saved my life.

There are other aspects of transition which you didn't even tangentially ask about, so I won't go into them all, but just to name a few: There's the social side - telling one's friends (and, generally, losing most of them); telling one's family; losing any spouse and children that one might have. There's the clothing side, presenting as oneself regarding attire, hair, make-up and so forth. There's the legal side, fighting with every single political and corporate entity that you had no idea even existed - I currently can't open a Verizon Internet-service account in my new apartment because, in my new legal

name, I have no credit history. Then there's the fact
that, as a woman who plays video games, I face a hell
of a lot of name-calling and hate speech from the
twenty-something males who inhabit the same virtual
spaces as me. And there's the fact that software
development, my profession, is at least ninety-five per
cent male.

I wouldn't trade any of these problems for the world.
I am so, so glad to have them.

CHAPTER 8:
WHERE TO MEET PEOPLE LIKE YOU

Do you like the following things:

- Holding hands?

- Kissing?

- Picking the devil mushrooms off your pizza and giving them to someone else?

- Sex?

- Hugs?

- Watching TV while snuggling?

- The idea of any of these things?

If you answered 'yes' to any of the above, then I'm afraid, sooner or later, you'll have to meet someone. You'll note that none of the activities are one-player games. Self-hugging is only for people in straitjackets.

As previously mentioned, LGB* people are in a minority. MOST people identify as heterosexual, therefore finding someone the same gender as you who wants to hug and hold hands with you is that little bit tougher.

Clearly, being trans has nothing to do with your sexuality. Some trans people will be gay, others will be straight. Later in this chapter, we'll talk about the specific issues trans people might have when meeting someone.

You probably won't BELIEVE this but, once upon a time, gay men used to hang coloured bandanas out of their back pockets to signal that they were gay and what kind of sexyfuntime they liked. Complicated much? Also, with rainbow-colour hankies dangling from their bums, you can only imagine they looked like My Little Ponies.

Luckily, LGB* people have emerged from the shadows. The days of gay or bi people hiding away in unmarked subterranean bars and clubs are over (although those clubs do still exist and they serve a function, as we'll discuss later). We have trendy bars and hip clubs for the over eighteens, and websites, organisations, clubs, marches and more for everyone – all designed to help us meet potential partners or friends.

The Look of Love

Ancient gay scholars (me and my friends) have often posited that there is a MYSTICAL SIXTH SENSE that allows homo-inclined people to sense when our own kind is close at hand. We are sex mediums, if you like: 'There is a gay in this house . . . yes . . . yes, the presence is strong now . . . he's definitely a gay.'

This gay radar became known as **GAYDAR**.

Of course, members of the LGB* community do not possess magical powers (or at least that's what we want regular people to think . . .). Instead, gaydar is a developed talent whereby we get good at reading body language.

How to hone your gaydar:

- So you see someone you like the look of . . .

- The first step is CLOCK THE STEREOTYPES. As discussed, stereotypes are stereotypes for a reason, and some men and women do have a 'gay look', probably BECAUSE we sometimes want to advertise ourselves to potential mates. A beardy guy wearing a leather harness IS likely to be gay (or a gladiator). Sadly, nearly all LGB* people are far more ambiguous than that, so we need further help.

- Look for SUSTAINED EYE CONTACT. This is by far the best gaydar at your disposal. I'm going to be super honest. Women (who I like an awful lot but do not like having sex with) mill around me all day. In passing, I might notice their super hair or something, but I don't really try to make eye contact. People, as a rule, make eye contact if they want to engage. If you see someone holding eye contact for much more than a second, or taking a second look, it's because they're trying to get your attention.

- INCREASED BODY CONTACT, such as a hand on your arm or shoulders, is another body language sign that someone is into you.

Very often, though, given that we're in the twenty-first century, most people just explain that they're gay. You could also just ask someone. How much easier is that?

These days a lot of younger LGB* people are out at school, college and university, so word spreads and you may well already know loads of other LGB* people already. Being LGB* isn't a big secret any more for a lot of young people, so there's no need for special places to meet.

For others, though, adolescence and young adulthood can be an isolating time, and you may have to be a bit more proactive to find people like you

Safe Spaces

For a long time, homophobia and fear of verbal and physical assault was so bad that LGBT* people did need special places where they could socialise free from intimidation. This is still somewhat true today. LGBT* people are not zoo animals, and as such we do not like being stared at. It's depressing but true that even some quite well-meaning straight people find gay people to be a bit of a freak show.

Because of this, it's nice to go to places where you can meet new people without having to bother saying, 'Sorry to ask this mate, but are you, like, erm . . . gay?' It saves SO much hassle.

This brings us to the concept of the **gay scene**, a somewhat out-of-date term which encompasses gay and bi men and women, and also trans people to some degree.

As discussed, being transgender has nothing to do with a person's sexuality, but transvestites, transsexuals and drag queens have often sought refuge from gawkers in gay or lesbian bars or clubs – they're not ideal, but they're a more accepting place than, say, Yates's.

A key problem with the gay scene is that nearly all bars and clubs are for over eighteens only – but we'll deal with that shortly.

SCENE QUEENS

Before we look at the various strands of the gay scene, it's important to stress that it's not for everyone. By that I don't mean heterosexual people, I mean US. Lots of LGBT* people do not access 'gay services' at all.

'I've never really had to engage with the gay scene because I've basically been in the same relationship my whole adult life. For me, I guess the gay scene may have had a slightly negative impact - I'd see all these people cross-dressing at gay pride events or big butch lesbians with French crops and very camp gay men dancing around, and I'd be like, "I'm not like that. I don't want to have to cut my hair short and spend the whole time talking about dildos and telling everyone about my sex life." It made me think that I was never going to quite fit in anywhere.

It was quite a relief to discover that you can go out
with someone of the same sex and then carry on with
life as it was before, without having to make it
central to your identity.'

J, 28, Brighton.

Many LGBT* people, especially those living in rural areas and
smaller towns, will not have the same services that people in big
cities (especially London, Manchester and Brighton) do. There is
no rule that says all LGBT* adults have to go to 'gay clubs' or
'gay bars'.

THIS IS ANOTHER STEREOTYPE. Let's all throw sticks at it.

Gay people in North Wales probably like mountain walking.
Gay people in Cornwall might enjoy surfing. Gay people in
Scotland build snowmen.

Here's another thing – LGBT* people IN big cities don't always
access the gay scene either. It's very much a choice.

For some reason – possibly internalised homophobia – no one
wants to admit to being a 'scene queen', even people who do
visit gay bars and clubs quite regularly. This is very silly.
**However we live our lives, LGBT* people have NOTHING to
be ashamed of.**

Let's not forget the benefits of having these safe spaces:

'Part of the reason I - a wee kid from Paisley in
Scotland - moved south to London almost twenty years
ago was because of the "gay scene" it promised.

London was very good to me, and I had a lot of fun in my twenties and thirties there. The benefits were having easy access to many pubs and clubs where you could relax, be yourself and, of course, meet ever-so-cute guys! It amazed me to be able to walk about in Soho holding hands with my boyfriend in public and not being laughed at, slagged off or even attacked.'

Aidy, 46, Margate.

'Being a part of the gay scene allows you to meet people and make friends that have a lot of the same experiences and interests as you do. It is also a really good way to find potential romantic partners. The only way I met all of the girls I've dated was because I'm involved and active in the gay scene in my area. The disadvantages are that it can limit your world view if you ONLY hang out with other gay people, and the dating scene can get a bit incestuous if you and all of your friends are fishing in the same dating pool.'

Taylor, 23, USA.

It's also worth noting that 'the gay scene' is probably more diverse than people give it credit for. There are as many stereotypes about the gay scene as there are about gay people.

CLUBS AND SOCIETIES

Obviously, you have to be over eighteen to go to a bar or a club, and as not all LGBT* people love drinking and partying anyway, there are an infinite variety of clubs and societies that allow people to hang out and meet. All parts of the 'gay scene' are as much about meeting like-minded chums as they are finding a partner for sexyfuntime. A quick Google search will unearth gay book groups, gay cookery classes, singles nights and just about every sort of fun activity you can shake a stick (I SAID STICK) at.

Erik, 34, London, is the chairperson of the London Gay Symphonic Winds – a group for LGBT* (and also straight) musicians:

Founded in 2005, the London Gay Symphonic Winds (LGSW), like many gay and lesbian groups, was formed to give people the opportunity to do something they enjoyed in a friendly and supportive environment without the fear of encountering prejudice. We have always been as much a social group as a musical one, and we aim to be as inclusive as possible without detriment to the musical standard. Because of our unique marriage of the social/musical goals, we have players of all ages, sexual orientation, and genders. The LGSW is a great way for people to meet friends outside of the regular bar and club scene.

For young LGBT* people, there are specialist support groups at young people's centres around the country. A fabulous example is Allsorts Youth Project in Brighton, which gives support to young people living on the South Coast. If you talk to staff at your school or college or look online, I'm almost certain you'll find a similar LGBT* youth group close-ish to where you live.

'I come [to Allsorts] to interact with other LGBT people. There's help and advice if you're struggling with certain situations, like mental health or sexual health, and it's a nice, friendly atmosphere.'

Lucy, 20 Brighton.

'I mainly come to socialise and meet new people, and they help with, like, if I got bullied at college for being gay there's people here that can help with that.'

N, 17, Burgess Hill.

'I like coming to Allsorts because, being trans, I find there's not a lot of support out there, and there is a separate group here for trans people. It's nice to have a safe space.'

Chezra, 19, Brighton.

As well as being a cool place to hang out and make friends like you, youth groups will also provide you with free condoms, lube, contraception and advice. Please see a list of active youth groups in the UK at the back of the book.

It's also worth noting that pretty much every university in the country will have an LGBT* group on campus. These are a fantastic way to meet like-minded people and a great way to establish yourself away from home should you go on to higher education. Each year there is even a STUDENT PRIDE rally where LGBT* students from all over the UK get together to celebrate and be proud and stuff.

There are also specialised group support meetings for trans people and those who may be thinking of transitioning. See 'Helpful Numbers and Websites and Stuff' at the back of the book.

BARS AND NIGHTCLUBS

If you live in the UK and are over eighteen, you are very lucky because I estimate you are never more than an hour from your local 'gay bar' or 'gay club'. Again, these are catch-all terms that can also include 'girl bars' for gay women. Some establishments are for (or will run special nights for) cross-dressers, transsexuals and transvestites.

These places are not to everyone's taste (and again, they only cater for the over eighteens), although larger gay scenes in London, Manchester and Brighton are more diverse and so cater to broader tastes. Issues range from the music . . .

'[The gay scene] is great if you like sugary drinks and bubble gum pop.'

Stuart, 33, Brighton.

to the clientele . . .

'There are a lot of nasty, bitter queens around most scenes.'

Dani, 29, Newcastle upon Tyne.

BUT the role of the 'gay bar' is historical. As mentioned before, they provide safe spaces for LGBT* people to meet free from ridicule or harassment.

People use gay bars and clubs in a variety of ways:

- **To have a good time.** Whatever music you're into, there's a bar or club for you somewhere. You can go with your friends and dance your little gay socks off.

- **To meet new friends.** Contrary to popular belief, gay and bi people don't always A. shag or B. scratch each other's eyes out on first contact. It is nice to have friends who understand what it's like to be LGBT*, because we all have some shared experiences, e.g. coming out, the hilarity of Grindr.

- **Sex.** LGBT* people cannot claim a monopoly on this one. Up and down the country, EVERYONE is going out to clubs to have a little snog and perhaps something more. It's the human mating dance, and we do it to David Guetta in sweaty underground lairs.

Most major towns and cities will have at least ONE gay bar or gay club. This is why rural LGBT* people often relocate to places with a gay scene. But no one is forcing you to. There are loads more ways you can meet people if you don't like bars and clubs (or are too young to go).

HOW TO PULL

1 Make eye contact. If prolonged eye contact is held, you can assume they're interested.

2 Approach. Start with 'Hey', 'Hi' or 'Hello'. If you're abroad, you may have to revise this strategy.

3 If they respond positively, ask if they would like a drink. (If you and they are of age and drinks are available.)

4 Chat! Compliment! Dance! When complimenting, always choose non-arbitrary things – things they chose, like their clothes.

5 If the time is right, move in a little closer. If that feels right, you could perhaps give a little kiss a go too.

It goes without saying that not everyone you find attractive will also find you attractive. It's that simple. Not everyone is to your taste, so you won't always be to someone else's. If you get rejected by someone you like, never take it personally – you're just not their type, and that's their problem, not yours.

'I met my boyfriend in a nightclub in Clapham. I'd seen
him there before, and we just started smiling and
saying hi when we saw each other. One night I saw him
standing by himself, so I just went over and talked to
him. We did have a bit of a snog, but we both had
friends staying over, so that was as far as it went. I
got his number and we arranged to go on a date the
week after.'

Jamie, 28, London.

FAQ: Why is the gay scene so druggie? That stereotype isn't
especially fair because what club scene isn't? Clubbing and
recreational drug use go hand in hand, and I assure you straight
clubs are just as druggie, but it can be surprising to see guys (or
indeed girls) in their forties and fifties off their baps on plant
fertiliser every Saturday. Maybe it's because most gay people
don't have kids back home and so can go a little wild. Maybe
it's because we're anti-establishment. Maybe it's because we
have a terrible Peter Pan complex and we need to grow up.

Just because it's commonplace doesn't mean it's RIGHT,
SENSIBLE or LEGAL. Drug use is none of those things. With
drugs, as with sex, it's ALWAYS your CHOICE. No one is
forcing anyone to take drugs on the gay scene.

Beware: illegal drugs are clearly dodgy at best, deadly at worst,
and you could wind up with a criminal record. St Thomas's
Hospital in London now charges some gay clubs a levy because
of the number of casualties being wheeled off the dance floor on
a stretcher. Not sexy.

MUTUAL FRIENDS

I think this one is possibly the best path to finding a suitable partner. What could be better than having your mates vet potential suitors like Sex Factor judges: 'No, you aren't going through to the next round.' 'You're going through to LIVE DATES! Congratulations!' etc.

Being 'set up' is often fantastic but also a potential 'mare of Elm Street proportions. PARTICULARLY when you first come out, well-meaning people (often straight) will bombard you with 'OOOOH, I KNOW A GAY GUY/GIRL – YOU SHOULD MARRY HIM/HER!' It is a sad fact that many straight people think having 'gay' in common is the stuff true love is made of. It isn't.

Other LGBT* friends or friends who know you well, however, can be fantastic matchmakers, especially once they know your 'type'. A lot of people throw house parties especially to mingle and mix their single mates and hopefully get you to bring some spare parts too!

Laura, 21, an MTF trans girl, and her partner started out as friends:

I first met Tess back in 2008. When we met, I was still living as male and in total denial about why I was so depressed all the time. We met when she and her group of friends came into the sweet shop where I worked, and we hit it off right away. We started talking

because she was a huge fan of the band whose shirt I
was wearing. We met up after work to hang out, and we
very quickly became close friends, but we were never
romantically linked. We knew what we felt was not
attraction but friendship.

Skip ahead a few years and my gender dysphoria had
hit its peak. I was near suicidal over the changes
happening to my body, and I just didn't want to face
the reality that I couldn't face living the life I was
living much longer. So I turned to Tess. She was the
first person I came out to about my feelings of
dysphoria, and she was hugely supportive, helping me
find resources and generally being there for me
during the earliest stages of my transition.

She was there during my trying to decide on a new
name, my awkward first attempts at presenting as
female and my first times going out in public as
Laura, all the while standing by my side proud to
know me, proud to be a part of the time in my life
when most trans allies are most hesitant. She was the
first person to switch to referring to me only by my
new name, the first to put her support behind me, and
she stuck by my side throughout it all.

Tess is gay. In the time I'd known her, she had only
ever dated women. I knew she had dated men before, but
since she first dated a woman, she had never turned
back. As I transitioned, our relationship began to
shift too. It became clear that while neither of us

had been interested in a heterosexual relationship with each other, we were interested in each other as I progressed through my transition. I know a lot of my hang-ups about relationships had been due to my deep hatred of my old body and the fact I didn't find heterosexual relationships arousing. Coming out and starting to allow myself some freedom with who I was completely opened me up to the prospect of being attracted to and in love with someone.

As I transitioned Tess started to see me as someone she found attractive too. What had been a great friendship, with sudden romantic and sexual feelings developing, didn't take long to turn into us starting to date. Two years later, we're still going strong, happier than ever and looking forward to whatever the future holds. She has been incredibly respectful of my boundaries regarding my body and has stuck by my side through everything, reminding me that someone in this world thinks I'm beautiful, even when I don't.

ONLINE

LGBT* people were way ahead of the curve with Internet dating. Long before the likes of Match.com was Gaydar and Gaydar Girls, named after our very own sixth sense. These websites – and now there are several – allow you to meet up with other LGBT* people for a coffee, dinner or sometimes plain, old-fashioned sex. It's very much a choice – and it's up to you to decide what it is you're looking for.

Now, pretty much ALL dating sites extend their services to men seeking men and women seeking women (cis or trans). In the gay realm, we seem to mostly use dating websites (like Match) for dates – with one eye on meeting a boyfriend or girlfriend. Most of them require some sort of subscription fee, but others are free.

Tips for online dating

- NEVER put personal information such as your address or telephone number on the Web (unless you like being murdered).

- It's polite to present a clear, recent face picture. And don't cheat with airbrushed photos!

- If you decide to meet someone, arrange a date in a brightly lit café or bar, not 'stabby alleyway'.

- Some people arrange to meet at their houses – be aware that, if you do this, you are inviting strangers into YOUR HOME. This is never a hundred per cent safe.

Be aware that many dating sites have a minimum age of eighteen, although some people arrange dates through Twitter or Facebook too.

'I've had dates (and consequently sex) with people I've met through Twitter, but they've come along as a result of my normal interactions on there rather than anything deliberate. Facebook is different - that's reserved for people I actually "know".'

Luke, 28, London.

APPS

The smart-phone revolution understood that, like anything in the twenty-first century, we'd eventually want to be able to download sex. It wouldn't surprise me if, in a couple of years, we can download the idea of sex so convincingly that we won't have to bother with the messy bodily fluids and pesky emotional stuff at all.

It is a fact that although grown-up adult types are sometimes looking for a serious relationship, sometimes they are just looking for a spot of sexyfuntime. You may come to establish that gay and bi men in particular do seem to quite like sex. OK, nearly everyone likes sex, but gay guys really seem to have cornered the market. Remember, this is fine as long as you're honest and always use a condom. Gay and bi men have taken to app sex like ducks to sexy water.

Technology changes frighteningly quickly (the lesbian app Qrushr has been and gone already), but it seems that market leader, Grindr, is here to stay. **Note: Grindr also has a minimum age of eighteen years.**

How sex apps work:

1. Upload a tiny pic of yourself to the app.
2. The app works out your location.
3. The app tells you who the nearest homosexuals are.
4. You then chat to them.
5. Because they are near, it is easy to meet up with them.

NOW. *Not* everyone on a sex app is there for sex. Like a website, it's just another way to meet like-minded guys or girls (there ARE lesbian versions out there). Once again, the app removes the need to ask, 'Hey! You over there with the arms! You a gayer, mate?'

If you want to use a sex app for chatting or dates, be VERY clear about this. In this instance, posting a pic of your nekkid chest would be somewhat misleading, no? Similarly, if you're looking for the ubiquitous 'fun' (the words 'sex', 'shag' and the F-word, ironically, are banned on most sex apps), be upfront about it and then no one's feelings are going to get hurt.

Most of us know at least one loving couple who met on a sex app and it became something more, but I'd politely suggest that downloading a sex app to find a committed partner is a little like going to KFC for a healthy meal – literally fruitless.

THE GREAT SEX-APP DEBATE
Pro sex app

'I have used Grindr - the advantages are you can get
what you want quickly. The downside is that its the
same people repeatedly, so can get boring very
quickly, and there is an awful lot of "Hi, how are
you", which people could do without. I prefer to be
more forward in those scenarios.'

Jonny, London E2.

'The benefits are obvious: quick, easy and
uncomplicated sex. On the downside, you always find
the same people online whenever you're at home, and it
matches you with people solely on the basis of
proximity - so the chances of meeting someone with
whom you have more than a physical connection is
very slim.'

Luke, 28, London.

'I've met a variety of interesting people through [sex
apps]. They are predominantly used for sex, though.
They're sold to us as "social networking" apps, but we
all know what they're really for. It's a bit like
selling a dildo under the pretext that it's sole use
is a draught excluder. I don't have a problem with
that aspect of it - if people want casual sex, then

something like Grindr is a must - but I've met quite a few new friends through it, so like anything I suppose it's what you decide to make of it.'

Stuart, 34, Brighton.

Another major plus to sex apps is they allow a degree of anonymity, so guys and girls who aren't 'out' can meet people this way without having to self-identify by entering a 'gay bar'.

Anti sex app

'After a long and slightly messy break-up, I briefly used Grindr and Scruff - thinking that it would be an easy way of meeting a potential boyfriend ... I realised very quickly that these services are mainly tailored towards enabling like-minded people to have sexual encounters - which isn't what I was looking for.'

Mike, London.

'I don't believe there are any advantages to these apps. I believe they are unsafe.'

Mica, 23, London.

'I know one guy who got gonorrhoea, chlamydia and syphilis from some guy he met on Grindr. All in one go, like a three-for-two special.'

Ryan, 32, New Jersey, USA.

'I've downloaded Grindr and chatted/sexted men on it
but have never physically met men via it. If one was
in need of a sexual encounter, whether it be a hookup
or something less casual, one could almost always
find something. However, the men on these apps tend to
be shallow when it comes to appearances and sexual
identity (i.e. "looking for masc", "white and Asian
only", etc.).'

Anon, 20, Minneapolis, Michigan, USA.

Using a sex app to hook up is LITTERED with potential risks
for which the makers take no responsibility. Tucked away on the
websites of sex apps (in very small print) is a safety section
which advises users to make sensible 'dating' choices. Yes,
everyone on Grindr is looking for a good, hard date.

In order to have the sex off a sex app you will have to meet a
potential partner, so this means them coming to yours or you
going to theirs. Obviously, this is very risky indeed.

As mentioned above, the anonymity of sex-app users means that
they have become colonies of cheating partners – a hive of
shitweasels, if you will. Beware faceless profiles. They're faceless
for a reason.

Some sex app tips

- Include a picture of yourself. Don't steal other people's.
  That's weird and shady.

- If you don't include a face pic, expect the first message anyone EVER sends you to be 'FACE PIC M8?'

- On the same subject, if you think your key selling point is your bare chest, we're in bother. Don't be a **prawn** – 'great body, but I wouldn't eat the head'.

- If you don't give your age, weight and height, people will assume you're old, fat and tiny.

- As regards all 'sexting', sharing pictures of your bits is not a great idea. Things do get shared around. Use common sense.

- If you're THAT HORNY that you want to do a 'sex meet', meet the 'trick' in a public place for a drink first. That way you can assess if you fancy them in the flesh / they are not a twitchy-eyed freakazoid before letting them into your house. This is much, MUCH safer, obviously.

- You can ALWAYS say NO. If someone from a sex app turns up and you don't like the look of them, don't be scared to turn them away at the door (of the safe, public venue you chose to meet at). Awkward, yes, but better than awkward sex.

- This one goes without saying, but ALWAYS WEAR A CONDOM.

- If you are on Grindr, under the age of eighteen (it happens), be aware that swapping 'adult' pics is actually illegal – you are distributing child pornography, even if it's of yourself.

DATING SAME-SEX PEOPLE

To revert to well-worn stereotypes, gay men are quick to jump into bed and gay women are quick to jump into Battersea Dogs & Cats Home, but as gay is now thoroughly mainstream, it seems likely that at some point you'll want to 'date' away from underground sex dungeons and drag shows.

Once you've met someone, be it in the street, bar, club or sex app, you'll need to get to know them better. How does one go about this? Like most people, it's all about wining and dining. Getting to know someone is vital because the outside package, however gorgeous, isn't going to sustain your interest for very long*.

*Excluding Jake Gyllenhaal. I could merely look at him until the end of time.

DATE IDEAS

Restaurant	Museum	Bowling	Cinema
Theatre	Walk/hike	Gym	Shopping
Exhibition	Gig	Picnic	Crazy golf
Sightseeing	Bike ride	Drinks/cocktails	Coffee and a bun
Recital	Sailing	Paint a mug	Wine tasting

Those are but twenty suggestions – feel free to invent your own. I think the ones where you DO STUFF, like an exhibition or a gig, are the BEST because then you have something to talk about right in front if you. Early dates can be tricky because at first you might not have any shared contacts, so it becomes a bit of a job interview, with each person presenting facts about their life.

That said, dating is so important to establish if there's anything in the pretty packaging that you like. This can take weeks, even months. There's no rush. The goal of dating is to establish if the person you're seeing is a keeper.

WHO PAYS ON A GAY DATE (or gayte if you will)?

For heterosexual people this one is curiously medieval – the guy always offers to pay unless he is awful.

But what if it's two guys or two girls? Generosity is mega sexy, so I think it's always nice to offer to pay. Your partner will probably say, 'Don't be daft – let's split the bill.' This is usually the way it goes.

If it was a good date and you'd like another, you can always say, 'Well, you get this and I'll get the next one . . .'

If you're in a food situation and your partner starts working out exactly what each person owes, dump them at once.

TRANS DATING

This is complicated. Clearly, a trans person can also be gay or bi, so some of the information in the previous sections is relevant, but some trans people will identify as straight. Being trans can be a complication in new relationships, but it isn't always. Many partners are fully accepting of the situation because they have fallen for YOU, not your genitals! Many transsexuals are supported through transition by new or existing partners.

Worrying about finding a boyfriend or girlfriend should never be a barrier that stops a person changing their gender. It's much more important to be who you truly are than to be in a relationship. When you are happy and content, you'll attract far more partners anyway!

Jane of Washington DC, USA, is a trans woman who dates mostly women:

(I use) Almost exclusively OKCupid. The reason for this is that it allows me to "screen" people who have an issue with transgender people. OKCupid has a specific question, "would you date a person who has had a gender change?" and another, "at what time is it appropriate for a transgender person to reveal their gender status?"

I don't know what ANYONE did before the Internet, but there are now a plethora of online dating sites especially for trans people, although, once more, you have to be over eighteen to access most of them.

Harrison from the UK identifies as FTM trans bisexual:

Personally I find dating has been easier since I came
out as trans. I am always honest, which I think is
something I personally desire in a relationship,
regardless of gender or sexuality. I found after I
came out I was more confident in approaching people
and even that it intrigued a lot of people. Some
friends have admitted to questioning their own
sexuality because of meeting trans people and the
possibility of dating someone LGBTQ.

The only negative experience dating as a transman I
had was that the person I was dating when I came out
- who identified as bisexual- had a negative reaction.
While I don't count it as a loss, I came to understand
that I needed to be with a partner that would respect
me for my lifestyle and that I wanted to transition.
At the end of the day I am transitioning for myself
and no one else!

Duncan is a trans man from Jackson, Mississippi, USA

Being comfortable with myself and being fully open
about my trans status means that I end up dating
people who are really interested in me. And if me
being trans scares them off, we probably didn't need
to date anyway.

Truthfully most of post-transition dating experiences
have been positive. The only negative things haven't
had anything to do with being trans, but rather just
not being compatible with someone.

CHAPTER 9:
THE INS AND OUTS OF GAY SEX

This chapter is about sex. Therefore it has sex in it. WELL, DUH. If you are a younger reader and feel you aren't ready for the finer details of same-sex pairings, then simply skip this whole chapter.

HOWEVER, before you do, I'd like to remind you that we taught you all about straight sex when you were TEN YEARS OLD during year 6. The fact that they didn't also teach you what same-sex couples do is nothing less than institutionalised homophobia. Straight sex was presented as the norm to make five per cent of the population feel abnormal. Is there something icky about gay sex? Is there something wrong with it? I challenge any politician to discuss this with me. I WILL RUIN THEM.

This chapter is simply all the stuff teachers SHOULD be saying if they want to be inclusive of people with same-sex feelings.

When I was a tiny proto-gay, the idea of two men or two women having sex was hilariously funny. I ascertained at quite a young age that a boy had to pop his peen inside a lady-locket in order to make a baby happen. That made sense. What didn't make sense was how two men could possibly enjoy making the ends of their penises meet in the middle, or what joy two women could garner from rubbing their front bums together. Surely the friction alone would spark a small fire.

I, for real, used to think that 'bumming' was the act of bouncing bottoms together like a fleshy pillow fight. I was confused at how such a wholesome activity could cause such outrage and disdain.

My confusion, I'm sure you'll agree, was delightfully innocent but actually hinted at something much darker.

Once upon a time, there was a very bad lady – let's, for the sake of argument, call her Maggie. She decreed that teachers must not include 'gay lifestyles' in sex education lessons. This was called 'Section 28', and it explains why I, as a young gay man, had no idea what a gay man was OR what they did.

Some years later, a slightly less evil man – let's call him Tony – took this piece of legislation away. That was good because now teachers COULD talk about being gay in schools.

Only one problem: Lots still didn't because they weren't told exactly what they should say to young people. Teachers aren't given scripts. Very often, teachers still sidestep the subject entirely because they're scared they're being 'inappropriate'. How can teaching THOUSANDS of young LGB* people in schools how to have safe, healthy sexual relationships be 'inappropriate'?

'My school was deeply conservative, and the entire extent of our sex education was to shock us out of sexual behaviour by showing us stacks of photographs of diseased genitalia. Somehow this didn't violate their "no pornography" policy; maybe it doesn't count as porn if the sight of it makes you want to dry-retch. The existence of LGBT* people was ignored.'

Stephen, 22, Johannesburg.

Lucky for the UNIVERSE, therefore, that I have no shame and will happily fill you in (ooh er) on all the ins and outs of 'gay sex'.

A Word on Porn

My earliest sexual experiences were some of the most scary, embarrassing, nightmare-inducing incidents I dread to think about. I was so unprepared. You think watching as much porn as your eyes can take will help - believe me, it doesn't.

James, 20, London.

Let's get one thing straight: pornography is NOT sex education. That is true of all porn – gay, straight, lesbian, whatever. Here's why:

> 1. Porn stars are expert sex-doers. No one expects you to be able to do that – especially not when you're learning.

> 2. Porn doesn't reflect real life. If men in the army were having as much sex as gay porn suggests, the world would be in great peril.

> 3. Porn stars are selected on the basis of their fantastic bodies, huge willies and fake boobs. Not many people look like that in real life, and you probably wouldn't want to hang out with those who did.

> 4. If all gay women really had fingernails that long, A&E departments would be a lot busier with all the clit injuries.

5. No one is using condoms. You must always wear a condom.

Basically, porn is fine and fun, but it is in no way REAL. You can take ideas, but it's definitely not for beginners. Everyone, including young gay, lesbian, bi, curious and queer people, is entitled to high-quality, expertly taught sex education.

'Gay Virginity'

Heterosexual sex is taught as THE NORM. Not just at school but in ninety-nine per cent of TV shows, films, books, magazines and news stories. It's no wonder, therefore, that many LGB* people's first sexual dalliances are with the opposite sex. Ah, the feeling of being shoehorned into societal norms. Cosy.

Therefore, many LGB* people lose their virginity twice – once with each gender! Both can be equally nerve-racking, but this is how a lot of people figure out what their preference is.

'I lost my virginity at age sixteen. I was making a concerted effort at the time to prove to myself that I was a hetero male so that I could ignore my thoughts, and my attraction to women was all I had to cling to on that front. I quickly realised that while I was attracted to women, I wasn't attracted to them as a man, I was attracted to them as a woman, in a purely female sense. I like to view my losing my "gay virginity" at age twenty, last year. This was the first time I had sex with a partner who viewed me as female, viewed us as a gay couple, and was willing to work with me to have sex in a way that felt appropriate for me. This was the first time I had sex as a woman in my eyes and my partner's, which feels a much more real event to me.'

Laura, 21, UK.

'With a guy it was awkward. I didn't know what I was doing or what anything was supposed to feel like. I was really disconnected from myself. With a girl, it was exciting, it was comfortable. It helped that we were each other's first girl experience, so neither one of us really knew what we were doing. But we learned quickly, and it was just fun.'

Sarah, 29, Iowa, USA.

'On my sixteenth birthday, I went to hang out at a guitar shop near my house which I used to spend a lot of time at. The owner was older, and married, and we'd been flirting with each other for a few months, though till then nothing had come of it. On this day, however, I spent hours there, as I had nothing to do till my mum finished work. The shop was quiet, and as the morning went on we got more and more tactile until we were rubbing our crotches against each other. We managed to stop short of getting our knobs out in the shop, and he suggested that I come round to his house the next day on his day off when his wife would be at work to help him "wash his car". When I arrived, the car had already been washed, though it took us both a couple of hours to muster up the courage to do anything. In the meantime, we made excruciating small talk and browsed that week's Lidl leaflet. We carried on seeing each other for a few months.'

L, 28, Brighton.

Part One: Boy-on-Boy Sex

Here is a diagram of a boy. If you are also a boy, you are probably aware which parts FEEL NICE when you touch them, but here's a rough guide.

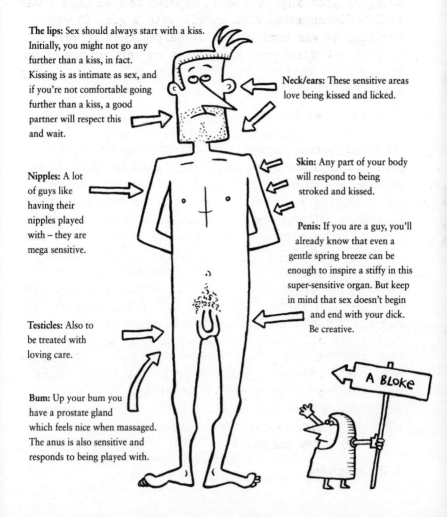

The lips: Sex should always start with a kiss. Initially, you might not go any further than a kiss, in fact. Kissing is as intimate as sex, and if you're not comfortable going further than a kiss, a good partner will respect this and wait.

Neck/ears: These sensitive areas love being kissed and licked.

Skin: Any part of your body will respond to being stroked and kissed.

Nipples: A lot of guys like having their nipples played with – they are mega sensitive.

Penis: If you are a guy, you'll already know that even a gentle spring breeze can be enough to inspire a stiffy in this super-sensitive organ. But keep in mind that sex doesn't begin and end with your dick. Be creative.

Testicles: Also to be treated with loving care.

Bum: Up your bum you have a prostate gland which feels nice when massaged. The anus is also sensitive and responds to being played with.

A BLOKE

Doing the Sex

Two men can pleasure each other in a variety of fun ways.

1. **Handies:** Perhaps the most important skill you will master as a gay or bi man is the timeless classic, the hand job. The good news is, you can practise on yourself. The bad news is, each guy has become very used to his own way of getting himself off. Learning how to find a partner's personal style can take ages, but it can be very rewarding when you do.

Something they don't teach you in school is that, in order to be able to cum at all, you or your partner may need to finish off with a handie. A lot of people find it hard to cum through other types of sex. This is fine, and certainly not something you have to apologise for.

A GOOD HANDIE is all about the wrist action. Rub the head of his cock back and forth with your hand. Try different speeds and pressures until he responds positively.

A BAD HANDIE is grasping a todger and shaking it like a ketchup bottle.

Finally, my misunderstanding about rubbing two peens together wasn't far off the mark – rubbing them together in one hand feels awesome – MEGACOMBOHANDIE (trademark pending).

TIP: If your partner is circumcised ('cut') you will want to try a drop of lube – remember he hasn't got as much skin to move around as uncut guys.

2. **Blowies:** Oral sex is popping another dude's peen in your mouth or, indeed, popping yours in his. There is only one hard and fast rule when it comes to blowies – WATCH THE TEETH. Lips and tongue, yes; teeth, NO.

As with handies and breakfast eggs, all men like their blowies served in different ways. The term 'blow job' is massively misleading, as you won't actually be blowing on his penis – it's more about sucking (although I stress you're not trying to suck his kidneys out through his urethra). It's more about sliding your mouth up and down the shaft of his cock.

Letting a guy cum in your mouth is a safe sex no-no. Get away from the volcano before it erupts. In fact, be aware that many sexually transmitted infections (STIs) are often spread through oral sex.

3. **Bumming:** It is a universal truth that many men like sticking their willies inside things. I suspect it must be biological. Well, in the absence of a vagina, gay and bi men make excellent use of the back door.

Wanna know a secret? Straight people have anal sex all the time too. Another one? Straight men like stuff up their bums just as much as gay ones. Why? As mentioned before, the prostate gland (located just up your bum) feels amazing when massaged. Lots of men, gay or straight, like how this feels. Anal sex ISN'T a 'gay thing'.

Still, unlike vaginal sex, a little more thought has to go into anal sex, and here's why:

Pre care: As pleasant as bumming can be, we must hold in mind that the primary function of the back passage is to do poos. Poo is not sexy. Therefore, those of you planning to have anal sex will need to dedicate a portion of time to ensuring poo doesn't creep into sexyfuntime.

The best, healthiest method is to make sure you've been to the loo before attempting bum sex and have had a jolly good clean afterwards. Poo is not held in the rectum, so there shouldn't be an issue. Some people choose to douche. You can buy a douche online or from an adult shop. Basically, this involves squirting a little bit of water into your back passage to clean the area out. It's a DIY colonic irrigation!

It goes like this: squirt the lukewarm water up your bum, hold for a few moments before releasing into the toilet. Repeat this process two or three times or until the bum water runs clear. Note: Bum water is not drinking water.

A lot of people don't douche. For one thing it's not very spontaneous, and for another some sources suggest more harm than good can come from washing away the bum's mucus lining (which protects the bum lining from tearing thus preventing some STIs).

I recognise this doesn't sound VERY sexy, but this is the reality of bum sex, I'm afraid, and a little forethought will make your sex sexier.

Roles: This is where dude–dude pairings can get tricky. At the end of the day, if you want to have anal sex, one of you is going to have to go 'top' (the one who puts his willy in) and the other 'bottom' (the one who gets the willy up his bum). Gay men seem to spend a lot of time talking about this. It's actually not a massive deal, as most guys are 'versatile' and will happily switch roles depending on mood, although there are guys who prefer to be strictly top or bottom.

Is the top 'the man' and the bottom 'the woman'?

NO. The whole point of being gay is that it's two guys. Being a bottom makes a dude no less manly than his top partner. Look at it this way: he's literally 'taking it like a man'.

How do you know if you're a top or bottom? It's easy – if the thought of having a big hard thing poked up your bum is arousing, you are probably a bottom. See? Easy.

Some guys are quite upfront about their preference, as this saves time further down the line and the potential awkwardness of winding up in bed with two confirmed tops desperately trying to convince each other why they might like to think otherwise. That said, most of the time, this can be figured out as you go along and, as mentioned above, there's no rule that says you have to have anal sex every time you have sex. Far from it.

Lube: Unlike the vagina, the anus does NOT lubricate itself. You NEED lube if you're going to attempt anal. This is for two reasons. One, anal sex hurts. The anus does not have the capacity to stretch in the same way a vagina does. This means it's a tight hole (which feels

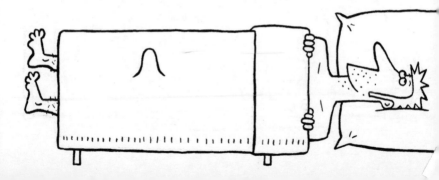

nice for the top), but it also means it can be very uncomfortable for the bottom. This is why lots of men don't like being bottom. With the right water-based lube, however, it can be hugely enjoyable – a good kind of pain like a deep tissue massage.

Two, lube makes it less likely your condom will split. The anus is a pretty fragile membrane, which means it's easier to get STIs through anal sex than vaginal. You really do need to wear a condom for anal sex.

P.S. A bit of spit, Brokeback Mountain–style, is NOT a substitute for a proper water-based lubricant, which you can get free with condoms from gay bars, doctors and clinics or buy pretty much anywhere. Vaseline and baby oil are oil-based and actually decay condoms. Don't use these as lube.

Finally, it's worth noting that some gay and bi men don't like anal sex at all. It could be that it kinda hurts, or it could be the fact that it's the hole poo comes out of, but some guys (and girls) just don't go there, and that's fine. NOT having bum fun doesn't mean you can't identify as a gay man, OBVIOUSLY.

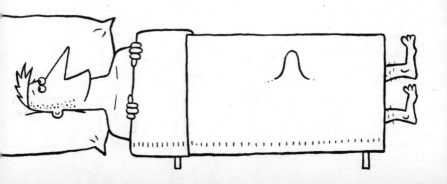

Part Two: Girl-on-Girl Sex

Here is a diagram of a woman. If you are also a woman, you are probably aware which parts FEEL NICE when you touch them, but here's a rough guide.

Clitoris: Observe the diagram. Women are that little bit harder than men, who have everything dangling out in the open. The clitoris is a super-sensitive cluster of nerve endings that, when rubbed, kissed or licked, can make a woman orgasm (which is a good thing).

Vagina: The vagina is the opening to the female reproductive system, from which babies pop out. Much, much research has been done on this, and it is thought there is a 'G spot' located just inside the vagina. Although the existence of this sexual holy grail has not been proven, many women agree that having things inserted into their vagina feels very nice indeed.

Anus: Although women do not have a prostate gland up their bum, some women like having stuff poked up there too.

Lips: Sex should always start with a kiss. Initially, you might not go any further than a kiss, in fact. Kissing is as intimate as sex, and if you're not comfortable going further than a kiss, a good partner will respect this and wait.

Neck/ears: These sensitive areas love being kissed and licked.

Nipples: A lot of girls like having their nipples played with – they are mega sensitive.

Skin: Any part of your body will respond to being stroked and kissed.

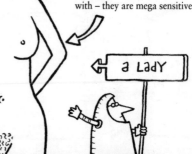

a LADY

Doing the Sex

Two women can pleasure each other in a variety of fun ways.

1. **Fingers:** Far more effective than a penis in many ways, a hand can do the job of five penises in one. When gay women refer to having sex, this is usually what they mean. Lesbians can stimulate the clitoris and vagina and bring their partner to orgasm with their fingers, sometimes both partners can do this simultaneously.

2. **Oral:** That clitoris really does like being licked and kissed. Again, girls can take it in turns to perform oral sex or, if feeling adventurous, they can perform it at the same time.

3. **Toys and strap-ons:** Some women like these, some don't. Much has been written about why gay women would seek to play with a replacement penis, but I say who the heck cares – if it feels nice, go for it! Moreover, a man is more than a penis – just because a woman wants something a bit penis-shaped doesn't mean she fancies broad shouldered, beardy, no-boobed men.

Toys, dildos, vibrators and strap-ons all fulfil the same purpose – a prosthesis to insert into the vagina. As with gay men, one woman isn't the 'man'. Two women having same-sex sex are both (yup) women!

DON'T TAKE IT FROM ME

Clearly, I am not a gay woman and, as such, why would you possibly come to me for tips on girl-girl sex? Well, quite. So I've called in an expert – gay writer, Fi Locke:

Let's talk about dildos: I think a lot of people assume that where there is no penis, a desperate sexual void is created, out of which something dick-shaped must ultimately slot in order to satisfy a vagina.

Basically, there's holes everywhere, but you DON'T HAVE TO FILL THEM ALL! Not necessarily even with your tongue (personally, I don't think that feels nice) and not with something penis-shaped, either.

I think most good orgasms revolve around the clit – well, for me and mine anyway! If you then want to get a bit fancy, there's nothing wrong with a few fingers inside (or a hand, depending on, well . . . y'know) during, or proceeding on from, some clitoral stimulation.

But that's orgasms. And as great as they are, it's not always all about them.

I've only ever slept with two women who enjoyed using dildos. I hate wearing a strap-on. I've only ever done it once and NEVER AGAIN! But then I'm more of a receiving kind of person anyway. (Also, strap-ons are really hard work! You need to be FIT to really shag with one of them! And don't ever expect to cum when you're wearing it.)

The whole 'butch dykes love strap-ons' thing is rubbish. I've heard differing opinions from friends and lovers about this which vary from agreement with the above statement to the feeling of actually feeling quite emasculated by a 'pretend dick'. It's totally personal. Some people love them, some people don't.

But back to orgasms. I love a good shag from a hand or a dildo –vaginal or anal – but, honestly, that's not about the orgasm, it's about the pleasure of being shagged. And sometimes that pleasure is pleasure enough in itself. That's not a timid 'It's ok darling, as long as you're happy, I'm happy' excuse. Genuinely, there doesn't always need to be an orgasm.

What else? Well, it's OK to ask for help sometimes. Everybody's lady gardens are mapped out differently, so if your lover is doing it wrong, help her out. Even if it means doing it for her once or twice. That might feel like you're just using her hand to have a wank with, and it is, really, but hopefully after a while she'll start to notice where you're putting it.

I've been with a lot of girls with this kind of 'This isn't straight sex, it's lesbian sex, and we're nicer and more respectful than them' attitude. That's boring. It's really boring. Just go for it and don't ever be ashamed about anything.

Lastly, I think you'll always have to take turns (unless you're 69ing). I haven't found an effective way to not take turns yet. Just make sure you don't do it in a 'Right, I suppose I have to do you, now' kind of way.

Actually really lastly: on reflection, I don't think girl-on-girl sex is any different to any other type of sex. If you just listen to what your body wants, what turns you on, and are never ashamed to ask for it, and if you experiment wherever possible, explore every corner of your desire, even if you only do it once, then you'll learn what you love and what you don't want and, voilà, you'll be enjoying sexy sex in no time!

Oh, OK, actual last thoughts:

> *1. Why do they always put 'veins' on dildos? It's gross.*
>
> *2. Note to manufacturers: vibrators do not need to be shaped like penises)*
>
> *3. Something in your arse, withdrawn shortly before a clitoral orgasm can feel AMAZING for some people.*
>
> *4. Lube is great. Don't worry about the sheets; you can wash them. Never run out of lube. Especially if you're doing anything with your arse.*

Who ever said that lesbians can't have sex? We beg to differ.

ROLE PLAY

Like gay men, some women prefer to role-play the more dominant or 'top' role, while others prefer to be a 'bottom' – a less active role.

HOWEVER, I think it's worth noting that the idea of roles is far from unique to men and women of a gay or bi persuasion. Many straight couples will experiment with power play as well, with one partner being more submissive to the other. Gay people did not invent this concept. Just look at that whole Fifty Shades malarkey.

For some gay people, the idea of 'top or bottom' or 'active or passive' is an important part of being sexually fulfilled.

'If it's for a quick shag on Grindr, etc., then yes [roles matter]. I don't use those sort of apps to have a chat or make friends. Its always better to be having sex with someone compatible with you in that regard, though. Wanking is something I do on my own, so not really up for just doing that with a partner.'

Jonny, London E2.

'They [roles] did matter for a while. I spent a few years experimenting with sub/dom. I had a partner who was strictly dom and would play games both in the bedroom and in public. Like, we would be in a restaurant and I would only be allowed to eat my lunch with my left hand, for example, unless she told me otherwise. Or a few times we went to Klub Fuk and she'd flog me in front of everyone or whatever. That's all fun for a while, but I'm a bit older now and it's started to feel a bit silly or boring recently.'

Fi, 29, Madrid.

'[Roles] shouldn't matter, however people are wired different ways. Some people regard certain sexual acts as either preferences or necessities. If someone can only be aroused by being dominated, then it's good that they're open about that in order to find someone who will fulfil that need.'

Stuart, 33, UK.

TRANS SEX

The sex lives of trans people can be a little more complicated than most, but they need not be. **There is one important thing to remember – people don't fall in love with genitalia.**

As most transsexuals living in their preferred gender are upfront about this, either when meeting people or online, their partners enter into relationships knowing full well what rudie bits their new paramour possesses; therefore, it's not an issue. Some people actively seek trans partners – both pre- and post-op.

Some trans people can opt for genital surgery, while others prefer not to, so this will obviously affect a person's sex life.

The same smorgasbord of sexual activities is available to trans people as to gay or straight people. Any hole's a goal (just kidding!) and everywhere feels nice.

Sex between women is very different than heterosexual sex. There's no pre-arranged goal of ejaculation and orgasm. So I think dating women, as a woman, is in that sense easier -- the sex is a little more casual. Where does the line between kissing or even talking and sex begin? We in the kink community are aware that there are a multitude of ways people can "have sex" and achieve gratification without touching, and without orgasm. So this is all very fuzzy.

However, I think that applies to the •lesbian• experience more than to the transgender woman experience. Your mileage may vary.

There's also the fetishization of (particularly) transwomen. If you look at the personals on Craigslist, you will see various sections, w4m, m4w, w4w, and so on. But there's also t4m and m4t. The problem with this is that there are men out there who I assume are curious about sex-with-men and so seek out women (which feels safe and normal to them) who have penises (which indulges their curiosity about sex with men). But I am not a man. And my sexual "response profile" is very different than a man. That tissue that men are familiar with, it doesn't work the same on a transwoman. My emotional response is different. So these personals and dating sites particularly for "trans" people (to include crossdressers and drag queens, the post-op, pre-op, and non-op trans people, etc etc), are almost entirely about fetishization. Which I don't want. I want to be treated as a woman.

Jane, Washington, USA.

But, seriously, whoever you are, whatever gender you identify with and however many labels you wear, there are two rules to good sex:

1. Do what feels nice.

2. Communicate with your partner. (How else are you going to find out what feels nice for him or her, and how would they know what feels nice for you?)

Why are gay men so slutty?

Well, first of all, I don't like the word 'slutty', so let's rephrase that to it's proper word, 'PROMISCUOUS', which basically means 'has sex with multiple partners'. Second of all, anyone who suggests that all gay men are promiscuous is a raging homophobe.

HOWEVER, the fact of the matter is that many stereotypes have a seed of truth lurking under all the horse crap. In this instance, both my own research and that of other writers suggests that gay men do seem inclined to promiscuity. In my survey, ONLY gay men reported having more than twenty partners in their lifetime, with several reporting they had had sex with more than a hundred.

This is not meant to be shocking. It is simply a fact. Remember, as young gay people, we were raised on HETERONORMATIVE VALUES, which means the values of the straight people who are in the majority.

Until very, very recently, same-sex couples couldn't even get married, so OF COURSE LGB* people haven't always played by the same rules as our heterosexual brothers and sisters. The gay scene has its own norms, and one of those norms, it seems, is promiscuity.

Some theories about gay male promiscuity:

> 1. **BOYS WILL BE BOYS:** We (and that's all of us, women too) get the RAGING HORN because of TESTOSTERONE – a hormone. Men make more of it than women. Fact. From an evolutionary perspective, a male could make about fifty

babies in the time it takes a female to have one. It is thought that monogamy (having one sexual partner) stems from our prehistoric need to have a male hunter-gatherer handy to help provide for a female's offspring. Basically, the only reason straight men aren't having as much sex as gay ones is because their girlfriends would have them out on the street in a heartbeat.

This theory is somewhat supported by research that suggests men are more likely to cheat than women.

Well, imagine women are removed from the equation – like-minded gay men can have all the sex they like, without the risk of falling pregnant.

This does not excuse bad behaviour. As higher mammals, we have evolved beyond simply reacting to the chemicals in our bodies and we are not ruled by them. No man, gay or straight, HAS to be promiscuous or a shady cheater.

2. **NORMALISED BEHAVIOURS:** Promiscuity is perhaps most associated with the larger 'gay scenes' – cities and towns where a lot of gay men tend to live. Within gay subcultures, men are supportive and non-judgemental of promiscuity; therefore, it becomes a social norm. Again, this does not excuse bad behaviour such as cheating on a partner or having lots and lots of unsafe sex.

3. **MISOGYNY:** Years of sexist dung has embedded the idea that promiscuous men are legends and promiscuous women should be dragged through the village square tied to the back of cart dressed as Moll Flanders (look it up). Men, gay or straight, are not subjected to the same

'shaming' as women, although I would argue that this is changing – everyone sees sleeping around as a little tacky, even gay men who are doing so, paradoxically.

I also wonder why, if straight men look like dogs if they treat women badly, gay men are seen (wrongly) as 'tough' and can treat each other as badly as they like. Women tend to frown on promiscuous straight men, but are often non-judgemental of promiscuous gay ones.

American therapist Alan Downs talks a lot about promiscuity in his book *The Velvet Rage*, which you could read if you're interested in this sort of thing. He writes only about gay men but believes (some) gay men behave the way they do because of an internalised homophobia that he calls 'shame'.

Feeling we're weird and wrong (which goes back to the 'different' and 'not normal' labels) has, he says, led us to believe we are unlovable, so we act that out in various ways, one of which is casual sex with multiple partners. He believes we are seeking external validation through physical acceptance by sexual partners. Doctors and nurses in sexual health clinics would probably agree that SOME gay men's attitudes towards sex are unhealthy. For whatever reason, gay men are more predisposed to addiction problems, including 'sex addiction', but that is not ALL gay men.

I am less sure than Alan Downs. There is nothing wrong with having multiple sexual partners. GASP – BURN THE HERETIC! I know, right? If all partners are **honest, open and safe** about their lifestyle choices, it makes no difference how many sexual partners you have – but don't go picking on someone else's patch, mind! No one likes a boyfriend- or girlfriend-pinching magpie!

It's about CHOICES, and I believe everyone should be able to live the way they want to live as long as they *don't hurt anyone else* OR THEMSELVES in the process. You can choose to be promiscuous or you can choose not to be. Regardless of how many partners your mates have, regardless of your raging horn, regardless of how many offers you get . . . the CHOICE is always yours.

BUT YOU MUST ALWAYS PRACTISE SAFE SEX.

And now for the bad news. **The more sexual partners you have, the more likely you are to pick up an STI.** There are numerous ones out there, some worse than others; most are treatable and all are avoidable.

A little slice of good news: statistically, gay women are at a low risk of STIs as long as they make sure any toys are cleaned (and you can put condoms on them too).

Infections that can be transmitted by blood, however, can be passed, in theory, through bleeding gums or cuts on fingers. No one is ever risk free (something to think about before you cheat on a partner).

More bad news: statistically speaking, gay men are in a high-risk category. This is mainly down to promiscuity on the gay scene. Hey! Don't shoot the messenger! Again, the more partners you have, the more likely you are to get an STI.

Get ready to feel some hi-intensity psychosomatic itching! Let's take a look at some common STIs:

1. **Genital herpes:** Nasty, painful and itchy sores on your penis, vagina, mouth or anus. Basically, a cold sore on the knob or fee-fee. Cannot be cured (you'll carry a dormant version of the virus for life) but can be treated. Once infected, victims may well experience further itchy/painful episodes.

2. **Gonorrhoea:** Although this infection is not always symptomatic, the most pressing symptom is a burning sensation when you pee. Some sufferers may also get a delightful pus-like discharge from the penis or vagina. As the infection is bacterial, it can be treated with antibiotics, although doctors are becoming increasingly worried about this infection's resistance to treatment.

3. **Genital warts:** Genital warts are caused by a virus called HPV, which is present in about thirty per cent of all sexually active people. It's highly contagious but, of the people who have it, only about three per cent will ever

develop a wart on the penis, vagina or anus. Visible warts can be treated with wart-removal cream, cryotherapy (freezing them off), excision (cutting them off – ouch!) or electro- or laser therapy (to burn them off). As if those methods weren't pleasant enough, the virus remains forever and recurrence is possible.

4. **Syphilis:** Large, non-itchy, non-painful ulcers on the genitals or anus are the first sign of syphilis. This one needs to be treated quickly with antibiotics or there could be secondary symptoms. If left untreated, it can affect the brain, eventually leading to death. Cheery.

5. **Crabs:** This one is confusing. WHY would you have crabs down there? Turns out 'crabs' is a name for 'pubic lice' – sort of nits for your pubes. You can see them AND they're super itchy. They can be treated with a lotion, but they can be a bugger to get rid of. As well as the itching, crabs have the embarrassing side effect of your having to confess to your parents, because the lice can live on bedding, clothes and towels. Therefore, affected items need to be boil washed before you potentially give your mum crabs.

6. **Chlamydia:** In about fifty per cent of cases, you might experience a slight discharge or a burning sensation when you pee. Or you might have chlamydia and never know it because you don't have any symptoms. The consequences for women are much more serious, as the bacteria can lead to severe reproductive problems. (It's worth noting that chlamydia can lead to sterility in men too). In 2012, 206,912 people were treated for chlamydia in the UK,

making it by far the most common STI in the country. That's just the ones who were treated too.

7. **Hepatitis B and C:** There's a whole alphabet of hepatitis viruses out there, but these are the ones mostly commonly transmitted via sex. They are infections of the liver and can be very serious. Hepatitis B can be vaccinated against (there is as yet no vaccine for hepatitis C).

HIV/AIDS

This one gets its own special section because it's of particular importance to gay and bi men, who (in the Western world) are the highest-risk group for this infection. Women, do be aware that HIV can be transmitted via oral sex, but you are not in a high-risk group, statistically speaking.

For my generation, being gay and dying of AIDS were cruelly linked. Young gay guys in the eighties and nineties feared coming out for this very reason, like we said earlier.

New cases of HIV are rising. How can this be, when we ALL know to use condoms, especially for anal sex? Two reasons: first, the nationwide campaign warning people about HIV and AIDS terrified a generation. Once the message seemed to get across, the NHS switched its priorities elsewhere – heterosexual people at far higher risk of catching chlamydia, for instance. This means that education about HIV is poorer than it used to be. The second reason is that triumphant breakthroughs in the treatment of HIV mean that people live with the virus for much, much longer (which is great, obviously – no one likes dying) and are therefore infectious for longer, coming into contact with more sexual partners.

This means we need to change how we view HIV (relatively few people go on to develop AIDS any more if treated).

What is HIV?

HIV (human immunodeficiency virus) is a hardcore virus that attacks a host's immune system, making it very hard for the body to defend itself from illness. AIDS (acquired immune deficiency syndrome) CANNOT be 'caught' but refers to the illnesses a person with HIV might develop as a result of their condition.

How do you get HIV?

You can get HIV by coming into contact with the blood or semen of someone else who is already HIV-positive. By far the most common way to do this is through unprotected (no condom) anal sex.

Can you get HIV through oral sex?

Yes, although the risk is much, much less than with anal sex. It is possible because people can suffer bleeding gums, making the recipient vulnerable to the virus through his partner's cum or pre-cum. Catching HIV through oral sex is very, very rare. But it can happen, so be aware!

Is there a cure for HIV?

There is no cure for HIV. Many HIV-positive people are under treatment to keep them as healthy as possible.

How common is HIV?

Around 100,000 people in the UK are HIV-positive, but – and here comes the scary bit – one quarter of these people DON'T KNOW IT because they are not regularly being tested.

Regarding gay people, it is thought that around one in twenty gay or bisexual men are positive, with this figure increasing to one in ten in big cities with large gay scenes like London or Manchester.

Numbers of new cases in gay and bisexual men are rising, not falling.

What is 'viral load'?

The term 'viral load' refers to how much HIV is in a person's blood at a given time. With the right treatment, most sufferers can get their load down to an 'undetectable' level, which means they are far, far less likely to pass the virus on to a sexual partner.

A person's viral load is at its highest immediately after infection and before treatment is started. This is when a person is most infectious.

What is PEP?

'PEP' stands for **post-exposure prophylaxis**. If a person is exposed to HIV, they can be treated with PEP for up to seventy-two (but preferably within twenty-four) hours after exposure. PEP is NOT a substitute for a condom and can have very unpleasant side effects. However, if taken correctly over a month-long period, PEP can stop HIV infection. It can be obtained at A&E departments or sexual health clinics, where they will assess your level of risk (please see 'Helpful numbers and websites and stuff' at the back of the book).

What can I do?

HIV is everyone's business. HIV doesn't discriminate between old and young, black or white, top or bottom, gay or straight. We all tend to think 'it won't happen to me' . . . until it does.

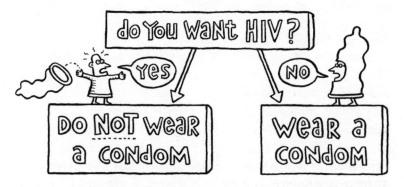

You might think that's simplistic, but it's also true. The best way to ensure you don't get HIV is to always wear a condom when you have anal sex. (This also goes for all the other fun STIs I mentioned.) I can sense eye-rolling . . .

'Porn stars never wear condoms' – Yup, but they get tested every month. Even then, a recent HIV outbreak shut down the porn industry, after a number of actors became infected.

'It's sexier without a condom' – OK, fair enough, but you might get HIV. Which is not sexy.

'He says he's HIV-negative' – he can't be sure. Even if he had an HIV test that day, that is only an indication of his HIV status **six weeks ago,** as that is how long it takes the virus to show up in the blood.

As well as always wearing a condom, **it's a good idea to have an HIV test about every six months** if you are sexually active. Why? As I said above, you are at your most infectious in the early days. Knowing early means it's less likely you could pass on the virus, and you can get on treatment faster, which is better for you too.

Your health is your responsibility.

KRISTIAN'S STORY

Every morning, I wake up, and the first thing I do after throwing the alarm clock across the room, is go to the bathroom, where I carefully place two bits of plastic onto my eyeballs so I can see properly.

Yes, I'm short-sighted. Shocking, isn't it? I mean, you wouldn't know unless I told you. But yep, I genuinely can't see my hand in front of my face without my lenses.

Being short-sighted isn't my fault; it's just something that happened to me.

And an hour later, before I leave the house for work, I tip four small tablets into my hand and knock them back with a glass of milk. To help my immune system cope with the effects of the HIV virus.

So there's two things you wouldn't guess from just looking at me.

Despite what you may have heard, HIV is no longer the killer it used to be. Sorry to disappoint anyone wondering if I look like Tom Hanks did at the end of 'Philadelphia', but I'm actually quite normal looking. Some might even say buff -- although my fondness for biscuits tends to put paid to anything resembling the six pack I had in my early 20s. Being HIV positive isn't 'dramatic' on a daily basis. But then again I've had about twelve years to get used to the idea. I'm not going to bore you with the details of how I got it. Had sex, didn't think about the consequences. Thought I was invincible. Wasn't. Was I a slag? No. Was I an idiot? Categorically yes. I remember getting diagnosed, back when I was 22. I wish I could say I felt angry, shocked, stunned, wretched, hysterical, whatever. I didn't. I just felt like a cliché. Another goddamn statistic. And for what? Half an hour of giddy bareback sex? Sitting there in the clinic. It just felt so...pointless.

Fast forward twelve years and life is pretty calm and mundane. I mean, right now, the biggest stresses in my life are managing my chronic insomnia and finding a route to work that doesn't involve sitting in my car for an hour and a half on the M25. Let me just make one thing clear, however: HIV is NOT a walk in the park. It's difficult at times. I've been in a monogamous relationship for the past three years with an HIV negative man. It required a fair bit of soul searching on my part before I actually bit the bullet and made a commitment to him. You see, when you love someone, you want to protect them, and exposing them to a lifelong virus for the sake of getting your end away requires a strong mind and an even stronger relationship. We cope. Our condom bill is huge.

Modern medication is excellent. I suffer a little with side effects, insomnia being one of them (see above), and diarrhoea being another, but it's something I've learned to live with. Like having a limp. As a single guy I was always upfront with guys. I figured if they had a problem with me being HIV positive, it said a hell of a lot more about them than it did about me. I read profiles on dating sites saying 'Clean only' and 'HIV negative - you should be too' and all I saw was fear and ignorance. You see, having sex with a positive guy isn't a death sentence. Actually, if he tells you he's positive, it's far more likely that he's health aware, on meds and therefore has undetectable levels of the virus in his system. To put it bluntly; he's pretty uninfectious. And when you take into account that over a quarter of people with HIV don't know they've got it, it's easy to do the maths. No medication means uncontrollable amounts of HIV, and a pretty infectious sexual partner.

If you ask my boyfriend, he'd rather be in a relationship with someone like me who's got his HIV under control, than to rock out of a club every Saturday with some random who might not know, or might not care. As I've said to many naysayers on Gaydar and Grindr in my single years - "I'm not the first person you've ever slept with who's got HIV; I'm just the first who's been nice enough to tell you."

Would I go back and do things differently given the chance? Maybe. I wish I could get rid of the virus and keep everything I've learnt from it. You see, it's kind of made me the person I am today, and that bloke isn't half bad. Living with HIV has taught me responsibility. It's taught me compassion. It's made me a lot less selfish.

At the age of 22 or 23 - whenever it was - I was wasting my life. I was checking out of reality in a haze of booze, drugs, clubs and sex. When the doctor spoke the words "Kristian, I'm afraid your test has come back positive', my world changed forever.

Living with HIV has made me grow up. After I'd processed the emotional fallout, I realised I wasn't going to die. Moreover, I realised I wanted to live.

I wanted to help others like me. And all of a sudden my life had a purpose. Sounds schmaltzy? Develop a lifelong condition and see if it doesn't give you an epiphany.

Nowadays I have a career, a relationship and a future. I do a lot of work in driving down stigma and raising awareness of HIV related issues. These days I'm proud to look people in the eye and tell them who I am and what HIV has made me. I get satisfaction from helping the newly diagnosed or those who are struggling. I feel pride when I look at what I've achieved. A straight male friend of mine texted me the other day to say he was taking part in human vaccine trials. He did it because my story had opened his eyes. I'm proud of that. I'm proud to have inspired people.

HIV isn't a death sentence. Like I said, my life is pretty normal and -- barring any wayward out-of-control buses -- I reckon I'll live a relatively long life. I won't lie and say that HIV is a barrel of laughs to deal with, but in many ways, it's actually made my life a lot richer. I really hope that one day we can find a cure. But in the meantime, I'd really love to find that quicker route into work...

THE BEST WAY TO PROTECT YOURSELF AGAINST ALL STIs IS TO WEAR A CONDOM EVERY TIME YOU HAVE SEX.

For oral sex, some people use condoms or dental dams too.

Saunas and Sex Parties

As this is a guide to ALL things gay, it would be wrong of me not to mention the things most brochures would gloss over. In big cities all around the world, there are places that cater to gay men's seeming obsession with sex.

Saunas, or 'bath houses', are dotted all over the country, and they are perfectly legal. People (many saunas run lesbian nights) pay some money to enter and then have a bit of a sauna and some random sex.

Again, this is fine as long as you're **safe**.

That said, NEVER ONCE did I hear ANYONE say, 'This is my husband, Derek. We met at Chariots in Vauxhall and it was TRUE LOVE.' Saunas are regarded as a little sleazy, and people often visit these places in secret. It is also true that sexual health clinics often have to treat people who have been to saunas and come away with a little more than healthy, glowing skin . . .

The advent of the sex app has also removed the need to pay an entry fee. In big cities, people often use the apps to invite a load of people round for a 'party' or a 'chillout'. These are code words for an orgy, simple as. Very often, there are drugs involved (which is silly because nothing makes a cock go floppy like many drugs – therefore, guys also have to bosh a load of Viagra. How EXHAUSTING). SOME sources suggest such parties are partly to blame for the sharp rise in HIV, syphilis and hepatitis on the gay scene. Geez, remember when 'parties' were about jelly and ice cream and sausages on sticks? Sigh. Let's go back to that. CLEARLY, going round to some random's flat with a load of guys you don't know is a bit on the safety dubious side. And, dear God, wear a condom. Wear two.

SEX AND LOVE

Homosexual people love a lot of sex, but we also love a lot of love. Every day, all over the world, you'll find gay men and women deeply, TOTALLY in love, and they have something better than just sex. They have intimacy, warmth, passion and LOVE – the NEED to be with their partner. Also:

SEX ≠ LOVE

You can have all the sex in the world, but it (quite literally) isn't filling the same hole. I believe we all want to be loved.

This chapter was all about sex, not intimacy. You can't find intimacy in a dark room or on Grindr. More valuable than bum or muff fun is holding hands, kisses and hugs. I'm sure some of you are miming sticking two fingers down your throat, but IT'S TRUE. Lots of LGBT* people don't even have sex but can totally identify as gay, bi or straight because of who they seek intimacy with and who they LOVE. By all means, enjoy sex, but if you go looking for sex because you're hungry for love, you'll starve.

CHAPTER 10:
NESTING

Q: What does a lesbian bring on a second date?

A: A moving van.

It's one of the oldest stereotypes in the gay book (literally in this case, which is quite meta if you think about it). Perhaps without men to make a mess of things, women are just far better at commitment. In any case, stereotypically, gay women are thought to jump to the cosy cohabitation phase at record speeds.

Of course, this, like any stereotype, has an iota of truth. All kidding aside, many LGBT* women **and** men do choose monogamous, committed relationships. This might be something you would like to happen now or further down the line but, however you identify, you have lots of choices about your future.

This decision actually opens a can of worms about norms, nature and nurture. Some questions to consider:

Why do we seek commitment?

How do you make love last?

Do gay couples emulate straight norms?

ARE WE BIOLOGICALLY PROGRAMMED TOWARDS MONOGAMY OR PROMISCUITY?

WHY BOTHER?

Even though very few mammals in the natural world form committed, monogamous pairings, humans do seem programmed towards it. Even the hardiest singletons seem to settle down in the end. There are a multitude of benefits to being in a relationship:

- **Love** – Sometimes the thought of being without someone is just too awful to stand. Being in love is like having a best friend supersized. Just make sure one person doesn't become your whole world – that's never, ever healthy.

- **Companionship** – Life is long and lonely if you do everything alone. Independence is vital, but so is company. Sooner or later, your friends may well settle down, and where will that leave you?

- **Comfort** – Yeah, going out on the pull is awesome, but so are cosy walks in the park and reading the papers in bed on a Sunday morning.

- **Sex** – Finding new sexual partners is a thrill, but having one partner who knows what they're doing tops that. Also, monogamy is much less risky health-wise, obviously.

- **Security** – Some people just feel happier and calmer knowing there's someone special in their life – someone who knows your Starbucks order without having to ask.

- **Financial** – If we're being cold about it, the system is set up to benefit couples of all orientations. Combining incomes always makes practical sense.

However, all these things combined don't mean anything if you're with the wrong person.

NOT BEING IN A RELATIONSHIP IS BETTER THAN BEING IN THE WRONG RELATIONSHIP.

Always.

I'm afraid it's not all hugs and snuggles. Same-sex relationships are open to all the same pitfalls as straight ones – cheating, lying, jealousy, abuse, emotional blackmail, bickering, controlling behaviour. What has always surprised me is how people will tolerate these things purely because they are scared of being alone or can't be arsed with the hassle of gays bars and Grindr.

NEWS JUST IN: THOSE AREN'T THE ONLY TWO OPTIONS.

We've already talked about how you can meet people and where to go on dates, but how do you convert dating into something more long term? We're talking THE LOCKDOWN.

This is the point at which you change your Facebook status, tell your mum, delete Grindr, etc. We're talking about having a PROPER girlfriend or boyfriend.

The lockdown is a critical point in a new relationship – I call it the 'poo-or-get-off-the-pot' moment. Basically, you have to decide if the person you're with is worth giving up the potential Gosling/Jolie waiting just around the corner. How do you know?

Well, this is why you date. People who try to rush you into lockdown need to CTFO. If you're taking yourself off the market, then, as with house buying, you need to carry out the full architectural survey before purchase.

Especially on the gay scene, surrounded by a constant stream of pecs, dicks, tits and mimsies, it's hard to settle for just one, but remember – if the person you're with is kind, funny, loyal, giving and loving, then these are things you won't find in a pair of big arms off Grindr or a cute ass at a bar.

PROMISCUITY VS. MONOGAMY

Both positions have pros and cons:

MONOGAMY PROS	MONOGAMY CONS
Intimacy	Lack of variety
Comfort	Missing out
Security	Routine

PROMISCUITY PROS	PROMISCUITY CONS
Variety	Loneliness
Freedom	Sitting at the freak table at weddings
Spontaneity	Herpes

Of course, some couples have decided to have their cake and indeed eat it. We're talking **open relationships**. A 2010 study of six hundred gay male couples found that about fifty per cent were in an open relationship, so it's not uncommon on the gay scene.

An open relationship is one with a cat flap allowing other people to drift in and out of the bedroom. Sometimes this might mean threesomes (or moresomes) with other people, or both partners being able to play away from home. All the intimacy with your partner, all the variety with extras.

Perfect, right? Cakealicious! Marie Antoinette would approve. (FYI, a lot of people think Ms Antoinette was #TeamBi.) You might question why everyone isn't doing this.

There is a very strong argument to suggest that monogamy is a societal or religious construct – remember how I said most mammals DON'T mate for life, and you can pretty much track the rise of monogamy around the globe with Christian missionaries (the same route, by the way, they took to tell people that same-sex activity was wrong).

It's thought that monogamy is the best way to provide a stable home for children, although this is a horribly outdated perspective in a country with a divorce rate like ours.

So why is ANYONE monogamous?

For one thing, it's the IDEAL. We didn't grow up hearing about the bit after the wedding where Prince Charming tells Cinderella he wants to be able to see other people. Certainly for gay couples with families, you can see why a degree of stability is best. Finally, as I've said before, I don't think it's ever entirely possible to keep emotions out of the boudoir . . .

At least part of the reason seems to relate to control. It's simply a bit ICKY to think of your beloved poking his or her bits in someone else's face. The mere thought is enough to put most couples off:

'[My boyfriend and I ruled out sex with other people] because our relationship was too unstable and new. We were both getting jealous and suspicious over nothing. Neither of us like the idea of the other doing things [with other men], even though we both felt we should.'

N, 27, Sydney, Australia.

'I've thought about [having an open relationship] a lot and like the idea in theory, but the fact is it wouldn't be totally safe, and I hate the idea of exposing my boyfriend to STIs. Of course I see other guys and fancy them, but you just have to accept that you made a choice to commit to one guy.'

Ben, 23, Manchester.

'There's no way I'd have an open relationship. I've been with my partner for eight years, and we have ups and downs but I love her and don't want to have sex with anyone else.'

Jenny, 31, Dublin, Ireland.

For some, cheating is cheating and that is that. Jealousy and paranoia are enough to make a peen shrivel like a salted slug or a vag slam shut like a clam – NOT SEXY. For most, having sex with other people is a deal-breaker and you may have to respect that or find a more compatible partner.

However, all people – gay or otherwise – must recognise that there is one universal truth of the universe:

WE ALL WANT TO HAVE SEX WITH LOADS OF PEOPLE.

Allow me to explain. We don't ALL want to cheat on our partners or be promiscuous, but – and please correct me if I'm wrong (although I know you're lying) – when we see someone we fancy, we can't help but fancy them! Short of scooping out our eyes with melon ballers, there's little we can do about this.

So it becomes a question of impulse control. If we all accept it's perfectly natural to have urges, we are, I'm sure, sufficiently evolved not to have to act on them.

For some couples, though, the idea of having to suppress urges is crazy, and so they allow each other the freedom to act on their desires.

In most open relationships, there are certain RULES. These often include:

- Safe sex only (well, duh).

- No anal (in the case of gay and bi men).

- Never in the home.

- Never on each other's time.

- No last names.

- No kissing.

No repeat performances (only one-off hook-ups).

Although, with so many rules, one does have to question how much 'freedom' couples really have.

JAY'S STORY

My partner and I have been together for eight years. We're civil partners, living together in our own place -

in short we're quite "settled" with each other. We're best friends as well as partners and know each other inside out.

A few years ago, we agreed that we could see other people, should the opportunity arise. It wasn't something that was decided for us to instantly run out and pull the first man we met - it was more "If the moment happens, then its not a problem." There are rules: we're not allowed to bring anyone back to our own home (unless we're together); you don't wake up at someone else's place; and we always tell the other person when something happens.

As for why we chose to do it, the first is down to the obvious: something new. As well as obviously being a lot of fun, sex can also be a learning experience and therapeutic - and one way which this is demonstrated at its best is in its variety. We realised that while we're still committed to each other and have total faith in one another, seeing other people not only enriched our sex lives but made us stronger as a couple. A further reason is that now, with hindsight and still in my twenties, committing yourself to one person for sex almost feels abnormal, particularly for gay couples, where (in most cases) the prospect of raising children and settling down in the traditional sense is non-existent. (My partner and I are strongly against the idea of having children. Ever.)

YOUNG LOVE

Lots of younger LGBT* people want to be in committed relationships – after all, that intimacy does look good, doesn't it? Well, it does, but remember, having no relationship is better than having one just because everyone else is. Would you jump off a cliff if your friends told you to? (ANS: How high is this cliff we're talkin' about?)

When I visit schools, most now have at least one 'gay couple' and, importantly, the rest of the school doesn't seem to give a flying fig. Schools are legally required to provide a safe space for all pupils so, IN THEORY, you should be able to have a relationship with a classmate. In practice, schools vary widely, with some far better than others at tackling homophobic bullying.

Outside of school, there's nothing to stop you having a boyfriend or girlfriend at all. Some couples I know in their thirties got together when they were at school and are going strong to this day!

This said, few people wind up with their childhood sweethearts, and not everyone is emotionally mature enough to have a relationship while still at school or college. Early boyfriends or girlfriends, however, are FAB because it gives you a taste of what being in a relationship is like, teaches you how to compromise and allows you to establish what you like and don't like.

'GAY MARRIAGE'

Finally! After much, much talking by many, many people, most of whom do not identify as LGB or T (begging the question 'Why do they even get a say in the matter?'), same-sex couples can finally get married in England and Wales. It has been such a tedious, unnecessary battle, but same-sex couples now have something dimly resembling equality.

Let's take a look at the timeline.

> 2005 – Same-sex couples are granted 'civil partnership'. It's anyone's guess as to why the government at the time didn't see this as discrimination OR why same-sex couples seemed so pleased with it. You might also ask what we were meant to do before 2005? The answer: be discriminated against.

> 2006 – The High Court rejects a bid to have a Canadian marriage recognised as anything other than civil partnership. BOO, HIGH COURT.

> 2011 – The Coalition government announces plans to introduce same-sex marriage before 2015.

> June 2012 – Plans are made to allow religious institutions a choice as to whether they carry out same-sex weddings.

> December 2012 – Provision is made so that no religious institution HAS to carry out same-sex weddings.

February 2013 – House of Commons approves the Marriage (Same-Sex Couples) Bill.

July 2013 – House of Lords passes the bill after three lengthy debates.

July 2013 – Bill is given royal assent.

For some unfathomable reason, it was decided that same-sex ceremonies would not be permitted in the Church of England or the Church in Wales. Man, it's like they don't like us or something. The good news is lots of other religious venues WILL solemnise your wedding, so it's still game on!

You'll also note that (as of early 2014) equality hasn't yet been achieved in Northern Ireland. They are massively faffing around. Equality groups are working on it. The same is true globally. Some territories are waking up to basic human rights for LGBT* people, while others aren't. At the moment, readers in Australia CANNOT marry, while those in America will be aware that you CAN marry in seventeen states, hopefully with more following suit soon.

For the most part, though, in the Western world, the tide seems to be turning in our favour. Rejoice! Whether you want to get married or not, I believe that everyone should be entitled to exactly the same institutions. The LGBT* community is divided on this subject, however – and with said institutions being historically pissy with us, who can blame them.

'I am strongly in favour [of same-sex marriage].
I believe that the halfway house of civil
partnerships was merely a stepping stone in enabling
full equality for the LBGT community. Love is the same
regardless of sexuality, and marriage does not belong
to anyone religious or otherwise - it is a human
social construct, and it should be open to all couples
who wish to commit to each other. Yes, if the right man
were to ask me, I would love to have a husband!'

Mike, London.

'I see no difference at all between gay and straight
marriage, and I can't believe in the twenty-first
century people still distinguish between the two.
Marriage is marriage, love is love.'

MJ, UK.

'I'm very much in support of equal rights for LGBT*
people, including marital rights. Same-sex marriage
has been legal in my country, South Africa, for seven
years, and society has yet to crumble. I quite like the
idea of getting married one day - mostly because I
love weddings, if I'm honest.'

Stephen, 22, Johannesburg, South Africa

'I absolutely support same-sex marriage. And I find
any argument against it absolutely ridiculous. This
may sound harsh, but there is one simple reason:
whether or not two people of the same sex can get
married has absolutely no impact on the lives or
marriages of anybody else. Literally not the tiniest
impact. And that's all there is to it. It's nobody else's
business, so there is no sense in opposing it.
Personally, I don't really want to get married, but it
is important for me to know that, if I change my mind,
I have the possibility to.'

Anna, 17, Germany.

'I actually don't feel very strongly about this. For me,
it's solely a legal/practical thing. All the fuss and
sentimentality is meaningless to me when you can just
get a divorce and void the whole thing if you change
your mind.'

L, 28, Brighton.

The bottom line is this: if you want to get married in England and Wales, you now can. Whether you're male, female, gay, straight, bi or curious. That feels right to me. I'm slightly pissed off that nobody's asked me yet to be honest. I'M SITTING HERE IN A WEDDING DRESS. The Marriage (Same-Sex Couples) Act is also fab in that it protects trans people too. If you marry someone and you or they change gender, the marriage will still stand under the law.

GAYBIES

Hopefully it won't come as too much of a surprise when I tell you two men or two women will need a little help when it comes to making a baby happen. WHAAAAAT? I know, it's true. You need a healthy supply of both egg and sperm, I'm afraid.

That said, this is but a tiny barrier in stopping same-sex couples from starting a family, and many are choosing to do so. Again, this is a matter of EQUALITY – just because we fancy who we fancy doesn't mean we shouldn't be granted the same choices as the majority.

As with marriage, this is a contentious issue (who knows why, it's the twenty-first century).

'I'd dearly love to be a father one day. Being a single gay man, though, I don't know quite how that will happen.'

Stuart, 33, Brighton.

'I think people who think through the idea of children and then make a conscious decision to have them are always better parents than those who just have them because "that's what you do".'

Fi, 29, Madrid.

'I think good parents are needed everywhere; their persuasion is irrelevant other than giving a good life to a child. I would love to adopt a child when I have a secure relationship and financial situation. I would prefer to adopt than have my own. I don't like the idea of being pregnant, but I do feel maternal, and I know there are so many children out there who need loving homes.'

Blaz, 34, Bristol.

'None of the arguments against gay parenting make much sense to me because they basically seem to fall into two categories: 1. "Children need a mother and a father because they bring different things to the family" - this makes as much sense to me as saying, "Children need one musical parent and one scientific parent" or, "Children need one humorous parent and one very serious parent." Obviously, different people will bring different things to a child's upbringing, but insisting it must be one man and one woman seems random. The "nature" argument never stands up that well either. 2. "Children will be bullied if they have gay parents" - kids can be bullied for any number of things, and that's not really a basis to say those things shouldn't happen. In time, having gay parents will be as unremarkable as having divorced parents.'

L, 28, Brighton.

L makes a very good point. The arguments against same-sex couples having children are wafer-thin. There is basically NO REASON ON EARTH that we shouldn't have families. 'Oh, but they'll get picked on!' scream homophobic readers clutching their pearls. 'Only by you, you small-minded twonks,' replies the rest of the world.

Two loving parents = two GREAT parents, regardless of sexual preference or gender identity. Got that? Good.

HOW TO MAKE A BABY HAPPEN THE GAY WAY

1. Sperm donation: A female couple can use donor sperm to become preggo. The NHS recommends you acquire love juice via a registered clinic, as it will have been screened for STIs and genetic abnormalities. What's more, if you go through a registered clinic, both mothers will automatically be recorded as the baby's parents. If you aren't married and use a private donor, the mother who doesn't give birth to the infant will have to later adopt it.

'I have always wanted to have a family, and I
never felt that being gay would prevent that. I
met my partner nine years ago, and after our
civil partnership in 2009, we started to talk
about creating a family. We both knew that we
wanted to have children, but had not settled on
the best way to do it. As a lesbian, there are so
many options. We considered all of them - known
donor, unknown donor, adoption, etc. We discussed
each option together, we met with a family
planner and we talked with friends. And finally,
we arrived at a way forwards that felt
comfortable for us. My partner would have the
babies through an unknown, but open, donor that
we selected from a clinic in New York. Now, we
have a beautiful 18-month old daughter and we
couldn't be happier. We both work four days per
week, and both do childcare one day a week. We
appreciate the equality in our relationship and
that both of us are able to feel fulfilled
professionally and personally, as mothers.'

Charlotte, London.

2. Co-parenting: This is traditionally where a gay man
and woman team up and raise a child together – perhaps
sharing custody between gay couples. It's not always two
gay parents; one can clearly be straight. However, as
anyone who has seen the shiteous Madonna film
Next Best Thing will know, make sure you have a lawyer
handy to ensure that the arrangement is legally binding.

3. Surrogacy: Sometimes gay men (or women who do not wish to be preggers) will enlist a surrogate to carry an egg they have fertilised. In the UK, this is painfully hard to do. While legal, the system isn't making it at ALL easy. For one thing, the prospective parents can't advertise for a surrogate nor can they pay a woman anything beyond expenses. At the end of the pregnancy, the surrogate is not forced to hand over the child, either, which means the process is fraught with uncertainty.

4. Adoption: Adoption is now available to gay and lesbian couples in the UK, and local authorities and agencies are crying out for new parents. The challenge with adoption is that many children needing adoptive parents have traumatic backgrounds and will often have behavioural difficulties.

So as you can see, becoming same-sex parents is something you have to really want to do. To me, it hardly seems fair that straight people only need neglect a condom and BOOM, they get a family. Alas, them's the breaks.

Parenting, should you want to embark down that road, is the most amazing gift a human can give.

MATHEW'S STORY

Mathew and his partner started a family in South Africa but have lived in London for the past few years.

We were not unusual in our position of wanting to
have a family - I think that this is a desire most
people have to some extent or another. Our challenge
was that the only way this could be achieved was
through pursuing the surrogacy route. We knew it
would be challenging and costly, both financially
and emotionally. But our desire for a family was
strong and this pushed us along.

Having children with a surrogate mother broadly
falls into two categories - either using the eggs of
the surrogate mother or using an egg donor. The
decision to pursue either route has a number of pros
and cons and in the end we chose the latter approach
- that of sourcing a separate egg donor. We set out to
find three key people to assist us in our journey. We
needed a social worker to help us with all of the
legal requirements, an egg donor and a surrogate
mother. Additionally, we needed a facility to help
with all of the necessary laboratory requirements.
With the help of friends and acquaintances, we
managed to find a surrogate mother who was available
and met our requirements. Additionally, we made
contact with a helpful and encouraging social
worker, and through the fertility clinic and the
wonderful assistance of our appointed nurse, an egg
donor was sourced, as well as a facility to get our
surrogate pregnant.

Once all of these people were in place, we met with a
specialised lawyer who helped us draw up a contract

with the surrogate mother and all that this entailed.
The current legal situation is a little different
from what it was when we did our contract, but there
were certain requirements that we had to meet,
including undergoing medicals, financial assessments,
etc., for the adoption process that would have to be
followed once the baby or babies were born.

With everything in place, the clinic soon organised
the donor and surrogate and got them both on a series
of regular injections to ensure the synchronisation
of their cycles. Everything seemed to happen really
fast all of a sudden after years of thinking about
pursuing surrogacy and then months of planning and
organising. Eight eggs were harvested from the egg
donor, and we were called in to provide the semen
sample. A few days later, we had a number of healthy
embryos ready to be implanted into the surrogate.
With the arrival of the big day, we were both nervous
and excited. We were also very keen to ensure that we
had twins - after all it entailed going through the
surrogacy route, having twins seemed to be ideal
for us.

We were present at the insertion and urged the doctor
to implant three embryos in order to increase the
chance of twins. The doctor, however, was of the
opinion that the blobs of eight cells we could see on
the screen were of excellent quality, and the decision
was made to only implant two embryos. There would, in
his opinion, be a thirty per cent chance of twins. We

were hoping for a positive pregnancy with the dream of both embryos implanting.

Seven days later, our surrogate called to say she had done a home pregnancy test which had a positive result. A few days after that, she went into the clinic and a blood test confirmed the pregnancy. At six weeks, we went with the surrogate for the first scan. It was an exciting time, and our excitement doubled when the doctor confirmed that we were expecting twins. We were fortunate that the pregnancy had taken on the first try.

The pregnancy was a roller-coaster ride. We were hoping for the pregnancy to be viable, that both twins would be okay and that they would reach a decent term. Week after week passed with regular scans and regular contact with the surrogate. Two incidents required hospitalisation of the surrogate for a short time but, all things considered, the pregnancy went fairly smoothly. Our babies grew well, and we knew that we were expecting two girls. During this time, we started to prepare a room for the girls and attended a multiple-births parenting seminar which was informative and nerve-racking.

We reached thirty-eight weeks (considered term for twins) and had a C-section date booked. The night before the delivery, we visited our surrogate in hospital. She was excited and nervous - a feeling that mirrored ours. Early next morning, we arrived at the hospital, changed into theatre scrubs and went into theatre.

The delivery was quick, and we were handed one baby and then the next. At 2.1 kg and 1.9 kg, they were small babies, but perfect and healthy. The relief was immense. We accompanied them down to the maternity ward, where we were both booked in for the duration of the babies' stay in hospital. Our daughters thrived under the care of the wonderful nurses, and after five days and a plethora of visitors, we headed home with Erin and Ariella. Having twins has been a wonderful and very challenging experience. Both of our girls are doing very well and growing up fast. They are now six years old, and in grade 1 at their school.

We have carefully considered how we tell our family story, both to them and the world at large - we talk about our family having two parents, like many others, and our gay relationship has meant that we allocate parental roles based on our ability, which has been very liberating. While of course many people are curious or unfamiliar with a gay family like ours, we have generally found, for the most part, a lot of warmth and support, and our children are certainly very well integrated into their school and community. There are fortunately more and more children's books that break the heteronormative and gender-normative stereotypes, and this has been extremely helpful both to our children and to the children that they go to school with.

We first embarked on having children through surrogacy so many years ago, and today it feels like we are just another regular family, with the day-to-day challenges that most families face. What we do know is that being gay doesn't mean not having a family of your own.

CHAPTER 11:
HATS

When you first come out or go public with a new identity – be it LGBT* or a massive *Project Runway* fan – there's a novelty and, perhaps once the initial nerves are over, a desire to shout it from the rooftops. And you should, because, eventually, you'll be **proud** of who you are.

I'm already proud of you.

There are days when I think, 'God, life would be so much easier if I were straight,' but those days are few and far between. I love being gay. I love my freedom. I love making my own rules. I love that I don't have to keep secrets from my friends and family. I love being part of a subculture and a minority group. I even look back on the difficult years at school and feel sorry for how small-minded some of my bullies were. I look at them now and laugh at how sad and TINY their lives are as a result of that.

However, an almost cautionary note to end on:

YOUR IDENTITY IS NOT A DEFINITION.

You are joining this amazing global club filled with awesome people, but you are also just you, and you are **so much more** than just a lesbian, gay, bisexual, queer or trans person.

OK, you need to imagine yourself as something with lots of parts, perhaps a HARP or a SQUID. You can totally think of your own example. You're basically a HARP SQUID, and one of your tentacles or strings is being lesbian or gay, etc., but you have many more parts.

DO MY HARP SQUID QUIZ. YOU WILL REQUIRE AN HB PENCIL.

1. What is your sexual or gender identity? _____

2. What is/was your strongest subject at school? _____

3. What do you cook when you want to impress someone?
_____

4. Write a favourite quote from a book or film. _____
_____

5. Tell me one thing only your mother would know about you.
_____

6. What's your secret talent? _____

7. Who would play you in a film of your life? _____

8. If you could do any job in the world, what would it be?
_____

9. Who's your best friend (real or imaginary)? _____
_____

10. Where do you see yourself in five years? _____
_____

You are a complex, multifaceted person. Yes, you. Even if you spend as much time as I do watching *Next Top Model* while eating chocolate buttons, that is still part of what makes you YOU, and it has nothing to do with your sexual identity.

Some of your tentacles will affect your life more than others and, frankly, some are a little weightier than others. As well as being e.g. gay, you may also be Asian, physically disabled and a tap dancer. In this instance, the tap-dancing, although fancy, might not define you as much as the other three. This is called **intersectionality** – the study of how much these overlapping identities will influence your life.

However, the fact of the matter is, simply identifying as gay, lesbian, bi, queer or trans isn't going to get you particularly far by itself. Engaging with a gay scene is fun, but it's not a way of life or, for that many people, a career. If we're honest, it's probably not enormously healthy to spend every waking hour thinking about where your next orgasm is coming from, either.

What I'm saying is, now that we've sorted your identity, you're going to have to develop a life. A whole life, of which being LGBT* is just a little bit. Open today's newspaper to the job ads. I'm willing to bet there isn't a full-page splash advertising, WANTED: GAY PERSON TO BE GAY. 40 HOURS A WEEK WITH OVERTIME/BENEFITS.

I'm afraid that, alongside being LGBT*, you're in the real world with everyone else. So now that we've used this book to deal with your identity, we need to turn our attention to far bigger issues. Your future, your career, your family, your kids, your aspirations and ambitions. Your hopes and dreams.

Of course, your love life is a deservedly big slice of your life pie, but if you shunt the homo bit to one side, you're in the same dating pool as everyone else. We're all having the same heartaches, first loves, dumpings, WHY HAVEN'T THEY RETURNED MY TEXT moments, bad dates and great kisses.

This is the final message. We are NOT in a bitter war with 'THE STRAIGHTS'. It isn't like that at all. Yeah, there are some homophobic straight people out there, but there are also some deeply homophobic gay people too. Don't go out into the real world thinking all straight people hate you, because they really don't, and you'll only end limiting yourself to what are essentially LGBT* ghettos.

As LGBT* people gain better rights and higher media visibility, the divide between gay and straight narrows. A generation of small-minded people are basically dying and being replaced by teenagers who grew up on Will Young, Graham Norton and Ellen. Certainly in the West, although we have a long way to go, things are better for LGBT* people than they ever have been.

That said, I don't want you to be too comfortable. The hardest chapter in this book to write was the one about the political situations around the world – most countries are changing for the better, but some regimes are changing for the worse. YOU will have to fight that because, love him, Peter Tatchell won't be around forever. Yeah, YOU. YOU need to help. Back of this book: Stonewall, Amnesty, Kaleidoscope, Terrence Higgins

Trust. Help 'em out. With each generation, things are getting better for LGBT* people – what will YOU do to make sure this continues to happen?

I like to think that, before long, you'll introduce yourself as 'a dancer', 'a fan', 'a friend', 'a writer' or 'a personal trainer' before, 'I'm Bob and I'm gay.' Straight people never have to do this, and neither should we.

Be proud. You have lots of different hats. Wear them all with pride. This is such an exciting time to be LGBT* – things are constantly changing and evolving and I, for one, can't wait to see what happens next.

CHAPTER 12:
A GUIDE TO RECOGNISING YOUR GAY SAINTS

As an individual, you will have a wide and varied taste in all things musical, artistic, political and dramatic. However, there are a number of people (as well as films and TV programmes) who transcend normal celebrity to become something far more special – they become GAY ICONS – and that includes icons for gay women and trans people too.

As these icons are not necessarily LGBT* themselves, it's hard to say what makes LGBT* people take each one to our hearts. Is it the aesthetic? Is it the glamour? Is it the personal tragedy or overcoming the odds? Is it the kind hearts or open-mindedness to our cause?

Of course, part of the fun is making your own icons. Sometimes we look to our mums and dads for inspiration, and sometimes it's a best friend. You can't help but be inspired – who inspires you?

That said, there are a few inspirations we nearly all agree on, and they have become associated or embedded in gay culture, so you should really get up to speed, if only to form an opinion either way.

Ladies and gents, here's a brief dictionary of gay icons, along with some of their champions from Twitter.

A

ABBA – Swedish pop marriage made in Eurovision, itself a mothership of camp. **@mytentoryours – ABBA. Don't ask why, just sance (that's a mixture of singing and dancing).**

Buck Angel – FTM multitattooed porn star, film-maker and activist.

B

Beautiful Thing – 1996 movie written by playwright and screenwriter **Jonathan Harvey.** The film features an incredibly sweet love story between two young men on a London council estate.

Beyoncé – Look, if you are known worldwide by your first name alone, you automatically qualify.

Chas Bono – Not only did he come out of Cher's vagina, but he is probably the most high-profile FTM transsexual on the planet.

David Bowie – The most high-profile bisexual on the list and probably responsible for bringing genderqueer and androgyny firmly into the limelight. A true icon.

Brokeback Mountain – heartbreaking Oscar winner about gay shepherds.

Bert and Ernie – The *Sesame Street* couple finally 'came out' on the cover of the *New Yorker* when a key part of the United States' Defense of Marriage Act was struck down by that country's Supreme Court in 2013.

C

Cher – Oh, God, she's just CHER. CHER.

Chris Colfer / Darren Criss – Their portrayal of cute *Glee* high schoolers brought gay to mainstream American youth. **@charlieinabook – Chris Colfer: 23, author, actor, screenwriter, unfailingly kind.**

Laverne Cox – *Orange is the New Black* actress and trans spokesperson / icon.

Joan Crawford – If her turn in *Whatever Happened to Baby Jane* doesn't do it for you, her depiction in *Mommy Dearest* will. TINA! BRING ME THE AXE.

Quentin Crisp – Writer and raconteur who rose to fame with his book *The Naked Civil Servant*. The godfather of fabulous.

D

Tom Daley – The Olympian announced he was in a relationship with *Milk* scriptwriter Dustin Lance Black in 2013. Fantastically, Daley refused to label his sexuality. How modern.

Bette Davis – The other half of the *Baby Jane* double act and referenced in Madonna's 'Vogue' rap

James Dean – The troubled actor is regarded as having formed the quintessential lesbian 'look'.

Ellen DeGeneres – Easily the most famous lesbian in the world, Ellen came out on live TV and is now in a high-profile marriage to *Arrested Development* actress Portia de Rossi.

Marlene Dietrich – Bisexual goddess of the silver screen, known for her killer line in male drag.

Beth Ditto – Openly gay, outspoken singer of Gossip and fashion icon. **@charlieinabook Beth Ditto: unapologetic, inspiring, great singer & open.**

Divine – Riotous drag queen, died way too young. Star of outrageous films like *Pink Flamingos*, *Hairspray* and *Female Trouble*.

Doctor Who – Gay men love the concept of a guy who never gets old, never settles down and is always accompanied by glamorous young women. Can't think why. Also features Captain Jack Harkness, a bi icon in his own right.

F

Jodie Foster – A lesbian icon long before she came out officially in a very odd awards speech in 2013.

Stephen Fry – Much loved for his activism, wit and honesty about mental health. **@_Buachaill_Dana – Stephen Fry, brilliantly clever, doesn't play on stereotypes & solely responsible for bringing Grindr to the public eye in the UK.**

G

Judy Garland – Considered by many to be the ultimate gay icon, Garland ticks all the boxes: beauty, the voice, the camp credentials (*The Wizard of Oz*) and a tragic downfall.

H

Kathleen Hanna – Leader of the Riot Grrrl movement and member of queer-friendly bands Bikini Kill and Le Tigre

I

Dana International – Another Eurovision alum, Dana was (and arguably is) the most famous MTF transsexual in the media.

J

Caitlin Jenner – The former Olympian became, arguably, the most recognisable trans person on the planet when she came out in 2015.

Elton John – The flamboyant singer and pianist is now known more for his activism and dedication to his HIV/AIDS foundation.

Grace Jones – Camp, eccentric, high-fashion.
A living art installation and foreshadower of Gaga.

K

Billie Jean King – The first professional sportswoman
to come out as openly gay, in 1981.

L

The L Word – Groundbreaking and explicit drama about
a group of gay women living in Los Angeles.

Lady Gaga – Although doing nothing David Bowie, Grace Jones
and Madonna hadn't done decades earlier in terms of music and
style, Lady Gaga was the first major (and also bi) pop star to
throw herself into gay activism.

k d lang – Gay singer and lesbian icon

Annie Lennox – As well as her past as a gender-bending pop
androgyne, Lennox is also a staunch supporter of HIV/AIDS
charities. **@adamswainston – Annie Lennox by far. A role model
for so many reasons.**

M

Macklemore – The rapper (WHO IS ALSO VERY SEXY) called
out the hip-hop world for its homophobia on the 2013 track
'Same Love'.

Madonna – Madonna has become something of a symbol of female strength: doing what she wants, saying what she wants, wearing what she wants. Gay men seem to like this a lot.
@MrSeras – MAWDOOOONA! I don't think there is anyone who has done more to encourage expression of the full spectrum of sexuality no matter what it is.

Ricky Martin – We all assumed he was gay anyway, but since he came out, the Latin pop sensation is the new poster gay for same-sex parenthood.

Armistead Maupin – Author of the bestselling and much loved *Tales of the City* saga, chronicling a diverse group of people in San Francisco.

Ian McKellen – Hollywood's most dignified gay actor, reaching millions in his roles as Gandalf and Magneto. McKellen is also a keen activist for gay rights.

Mean Girls – Dialogue from this film makes up eighty-seven per cent of any conversation between gay men.

Bette Midler – Gay-friendly diva who started her career playing in a gay sauna.

Harvey Milk – Openly gay city supervisor of San Francisco who fought for equality and the protection of gay people in their jobs. Assassinated in his prime. A true hero. **@BioLabMan – Harvey Milk. I could go on at length as to what that man did!**

Liza Minnelli – Not only does she possess Judy Garland's genes, but she earns her spot through her tumultuous private life and Oscar-winning role in *Cabaret*.

The Minogue sisters – Everyone loves a bit of sibling rivalry. Do you like the perky blond one or the sultry brunette? FIGHT. Kylie was taken to the gays' hearts because of her transformation from bubble-permed soap mechanic to hot-panted pop phenomenon.

N

Martina Navratilova – Openly gay sportsperson and the most successful tennis player of all time.

O

Rosie O'Donnell – Outspoken lesbian television personality

Frank Ocean – The soul singer came out in 2012, a huge step for a young black guy with connections to the stereotypically homophobic world of hip-hop.

Oprah Winfrey – Outspoken **NOT LESBIAN** television personality.

P

Ellen Page – The Oscar-nominated actress came out as gay in 2014.

Paris is Burning – 1990 documentary about the ballroom drag scene in NYC, giving the community a whole new vocabulary. "Category IS, cultural realness!"

Dorothy Parker – American writer and satirist known for her cutting wit and killer put downs – an inspiration to all.

Dolly Parton – A countrified version of Cher. A survivor who rose out of nothing to become a one-woman empire.

Andrej Pejic – Glorious trans supermodel originally discovered while working in McDonalds.

Pierre et Gilles – French artists and gay couple known for their flamboyant, hyperreal photo paintings

Q

Queer as Folk – UK or US TV show depending on which version you're watching. The UK version was enormously groundbreaking at the time with its depiction of gay sex and relationships and made a star of its creator Russell T Davies, who went on to revive *Doctor Who*.

R

Michelle Rodriguez – Is seemingly dating supermodel Cara Delevingne. The *Fast and Furious* actor refuses to define her sexual fluidity, saying, 'Men are intriguing. So are chicks.'

Willow Rosenberg – As played by Alyson Hannigan in *Buffy the Vampire Slayer*, she's one of the best depictions of a young gay woman on prime-time TV.

RuPaul –World-famous drag queen and singer, RuPaul reached a new generation as a mentor on the high camp *RuPaul's Drag Race*. YOU BETTER WERK.

S

Saint Sebastian – Often considered the very first gay icon. Always depicted topless, tormented and very hot. A muse to many a gay artist.

JD Samson – Moustachioed lesbian icon from Le Tigre.

Sex and the City – Created and written mostly by gay men, this series depicting the lives of four NYC women is now a camp classic. Samantha is bi, Miranda (**Cynthia Nixon**) is gay in real life and Geri Halliwell pops up in one episode.

Showgirls – Nothing is camper than this 'shocking' film about a stripper becoming a Las Vegas showgirl. Learn the script or you'll have little to talk about with gay men. IT'S A VERSAYSE.

Dusty Springfield – Soulful, tragic singer – the Amy Winehouse of her era. Also identified as bisexual and unofficially married a woman.

Barbra Streisand – Singer and actor. I'm not sure why gay men like her so much, but they really do. Especially American gays.

"Larry Stylinson" – *see* Tumblr

Tilda Swinton – Androgynous, mysterious and flawless actress. A muse to Bowie. Like Cher, she now gets away with 'Tilda'.

T

Peter Tatchell – This man has dedicated his life to gay activism. You might not know it, but we all owe this man a pint.

Gareth Thomas – Retired professional rugby player and out gay man. Every out sportsman is driving a wedge into a sealed homophobic door of silence in sport.

Alan Turing – Genius mathematician and codebreaker who won us the Second World War. Killed himself following chemical castration. A legend. @Gavin H – **Alan Turing because without him we wouldn't know anything.**

W

John Waters – Writer and director of camp classics such as *Hairspray*, *Serial Mom* and *Pink Flamingos*. Collaborator with Divine.

Sarah Waters – Author known for her use of lesbian characters in the novels *Tipping the Velvet* and *Fingersmith*.

Oscar Wilde – Mega-fabulous Irish author and playwright known for *The Importance of Being Earnest* and *The Picture of Dorian Gray*. Got himself jailed simply for being gay.

Jeanette Winterson – Lesbian author of *Oranges Are Not The Only Fruit*.

Will & Grace – It's not the funniest or most subversive American comedy ever made, but a prime-time sitcom about two gay men in the 1990s and early 2000s was a step in the right direction. Also KAREN WALKER.

As time moves on, some of these names will fade and new, exciting voices and minds will fill the list. Straight people don't get asked about 'straight icons', and it's not necessarily fair to expect famous LGBT* people to serve as role models for the rest of us – but I think those who DO are helping the world see us a little better. Here are a few lines to add you own gay icons.

_____

_____

_____

_____

_____

_____

_____

_____

Blacklist and Boycott

As well as supporting gay-friendly people and organisations, it's also important to blacklist and boycott people and companies who are homophobic.

- DO NOT download music from rappers who use the word 'faggot'. You're paying them to be homophobic.

- DO NOT see films based on books by notable homophobe authors (and don't buy their books).

- DO NOT pay to see comedians who are either outwardly homophobic or add to homophobic myths about the gay community.

- DO NOT travel to countries with poor human rights records.

- DO NOT buy produce from countries with poor human rights records. For example, at the time of writing many LGBT* people are refusing to buy Russian vodka because of that country's discriminatory stance against gays.

I'm not going to list homophobic singers, actors and personalities here because I'm not giving them the oxygen of publicity. What's reassuring is that once a homophobe has revealed their true colours, they tend to disappear from view.

It's a valuable lesson: no one wants to be associated with a bigot, least of all a record label or a film studio.

BUILD A BRIDGE:

GUIDANCE FOR PARENTS AND

CARERS OF LGBT*- YOUTH

Hey there, parents and carers – how's it going? Now, I guess there's a possibility you purchased this book because your progeny identifies as lesbian, bi, gay, queer, curious or transgender. Perhaps you bought it because you suspect your child may be leaning that way. Either way, I'm glad you did. You have come to the right place.

Being a parent of an LGBT* (that little star represents the full spectrum of sexualities and identities) child is challenging, but only in the way that being a parent is challenging. In the NICEST POSSIBLE WAY, this isn't about you. If you are really worried about WHAT THE NEIGHBOURS WILL SAY, then there's not really a lot I can say or do to help you with that, other than tell you to get over it. The days of keeping LGBT* people hidden in closets or bricked up in walls are over.

OK, let's break it down a bit.

Gay or bi son? Is it the sex stuff that's worrying you? Here's the thing – **straight people do bum sex too.** And two girls are pretty much doing what your daughter would be doing with a dude, I'm afraid. Basically NO parent needs a visual of that, so as a race we all have to buy into the shared delusion that our kids will only ever hold hands until the stork arrives, or else we'll go mental.

Is HIV/AIDS worrying you? It should, but you should worry about your straight kids too – HIV isn't at all picky. If you teach your kids about ALWAYS using condoms, however, you've done your job.

The BEST parent in the world would be one who prepared for having a gay child from conception, so that when baby comes into the world you aren't incorrectly tagging them as straight and cisgender (the gender they are assigned at birth). Be READY for all eventualities.

In the very beginning of this book, I describe overhearing a mother telling her infant that when he's older he'll 'kiss girls'. Well there's a five per cent chance he'll want to kiss boys, so that mother was potentially setting him up for a very difficult adolescence. All a parent needs to do is be HONEST and explain at an early age, in a totally appropriate way, that five per cent of people will want to kiss people the same sex as them. I assure you letting children in on this secret is NOT going to 'turn them gay'. It really, REALLY doesn't work like that. You could do a LOT worse than buying a copy of the gorgeous picture book *And Tango Makes Three* and sharing it with your child.

If you are a parent who is starting to suspect your child may be LBGT*, you would do a fantastic job to let them know how cool you are with that. Let them know, subtly, that you're open minded; let them know that you're there to listen; don't turn off the TV when lesbians come on. Yeah, that actually happens a lot. Instead, use gay characters on TV as a talking point to display your coolness with the gay community – that way your son or daughter is much more likely to open up to you.

If your child has already 'come out' with their identity, then reading this book will help. It will give you a glimpse into the future – the case studies in this book have been through it all before, and we all survived. What's more, most of us survived with our parental relationships intact, even if there were difficult periods. Unnecessarily difficult, I would argue.

But don't just take it from me. I asked each of the participants in my study what advice they wish they'd given their parents before they came out. Here's what they said:

'Don't force the issue, but take any opportunity to show that you are open to any choice that they want to make. My coming out was about as easy as it gets really, made that way by a mother who never pushed to find out but gave me an opportunity to tell her. Before you come out, it seems like the hardest thing you will ever have to do, and coming to terms with your own sexuality can take time.'

Chris, Manchester.

'Let them be. That may sound weird, but if they want to talk to you about it, they will. The best thing you can do is try to let them know that you're okay with it (in a subtle way, not saying outright to them, "It's okay if you're gay, you know"). If you're not okay with it, then it's time for you to think about that. Why aren't you okay with it? What's the real problem here?'

Kayla, 21, Winnipeg, Canada.

'They are still your child, just reimagined. Forcing them back in the closet because you are uncomfortable is a s**tty thing to do. Pretending they are still straight is a crappy thing to do. Making them go to a pray-away-the-gay camp is not only very s**tty but a mentally and emotionally scarring experience. The world does not owe you a straight child; you produced, not reproduced. Is your tantrum over not "getting your way" worth the relationship with your child? You are still allowed to have opinions of your child's partners, like whether they are good people, have goals, make your child happy. You know, like you would if your child were straight.'

Elizabeth, 23, Chicago, Illinois, USA.

'Educate yourself from reputable sources. Be cool about it, even if you're slightly freaking out inside. And ASK YOUR CHILD what they would like you to say to others, how they would like to be represented to the larger world by you. And then STICK TO THAT. It builds trust with your child and enables them to be comfortable in their life and progress at their own pace. Allow them to control their own narrative.'

Anon, 24, Boston, Massachusetts, USA.

'Wait for them to tell you. If you ask them, they'll
freak out. It's not fair to force them to come out to
you. If you really want them to trust you, make sure
that you create a space in which they feel safe and
comfortable talking to you. It is your responsibility
to make them feel like they can trust you.'

E, 16, Michigan, USA.

'It's a bumpy ride for any child growing up who isn't
heterosexual, so just listen to them. Allow them to
talk freely and openly about who they are and
respond with nothing but love and compassion, and
stress to them that there is nothing wrong with them.'

Stuart, 33, UK.

The survey respondents MAINLY swing to the do NOT try to
force it out of your child camp, although a few clearly say they
would prefer a more direct route:

'Sometimes asking outright is better than constantly
hedging around the question. If my mum were to ask me,
"Are you gay?" or, "Are you bi?" I'd answer honestly.
Since she's never done that, it's always been a sort of
elephant in the room for us.'

Stephanie, 24, Pittsburgh, Pennsylvania, USA

I think it's up to you as a parent to know if your child will respond well to a very direct approach.

As a final point, be aware that your child's identity isn't your 'fault' and, even if it were, it's no bad thing. I've been gay for a really long time now, and it's pretty good fun. To be honest, in my careers as a teacher and author it's had very little impact. I used to be in a band, and I did clinical neuropsychology at university. I got a first-class honours degree. My sexuality hasn't held me back EVER.

Your child's identity is a part of them that has always been there. They haven't even changed; it's just that now you're seeing the whole picture – IT'S BUTTERFLY TIME.

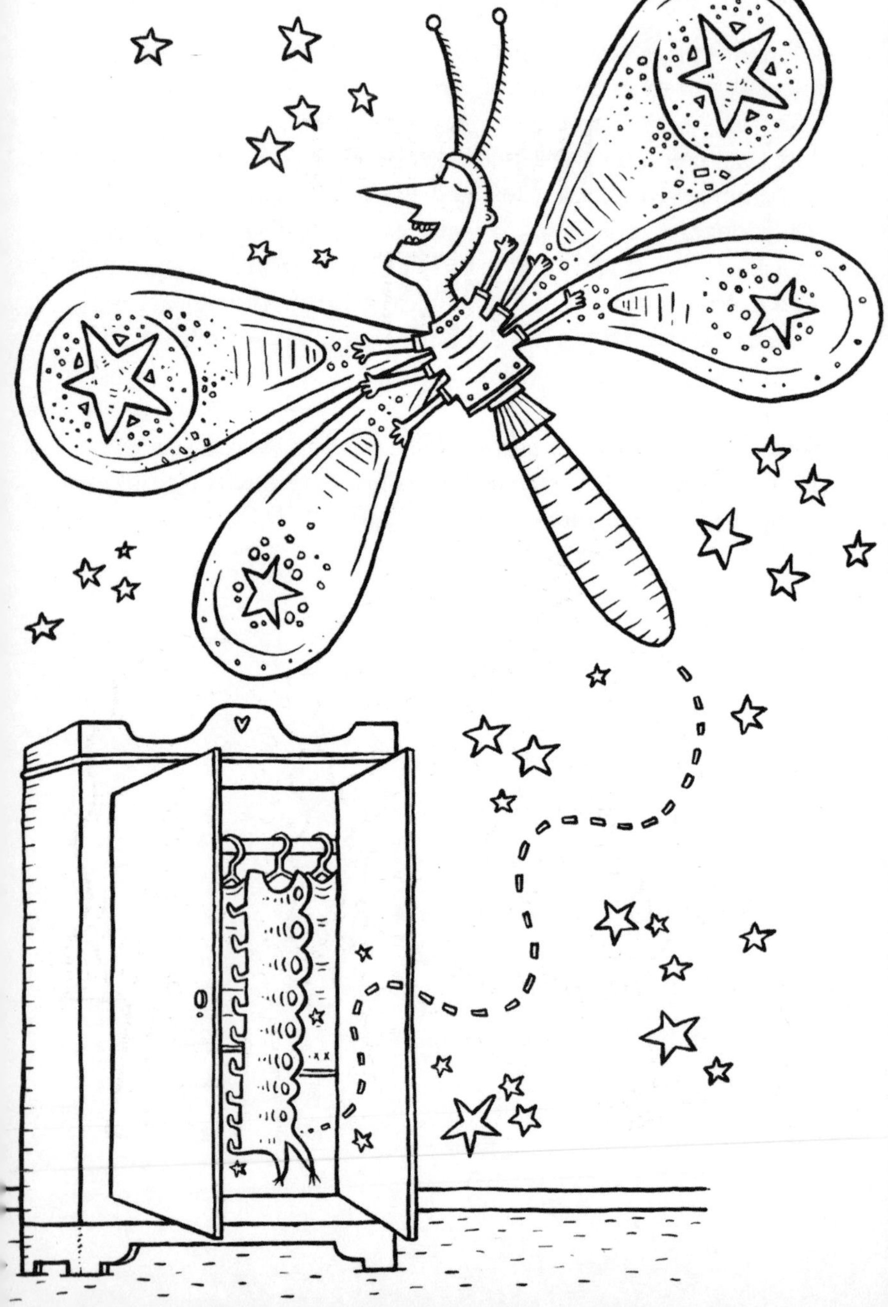

THE CHEAT SHEET

All the weird terms, no waiting.

69: *Two people giving simultaneous oral sex.*

AIDS: *A syndrome brought on by the virus HIV.*

Asexual: *A person who is not interested in sex or has low sexual desire.*

Bisexual: *A person who fancies both men and women.*

Blow job: *Oral sex on a guy.*

Bottom/passive: *Being the partner who 'receives' during sex*

Circumcised: *Term to describe a boy who has had his foreskin surgically removed.*

Cisgender: *The sex you were assigned at birth.*

Clitoris: *Female erogenous zone.*

'Coming out': *The process of telling people about your identity.*

Cum: *Common slang term for semen OR to orgasm.*

Cunnilingus: *Oral sex on a girl.*

Curious/questioning: *A person in the process of wondering about their sexuality.*

Dildo: *A sex toy.*

Dom: *Being the dominant partner during sex.*

Douching: *Washing out the back passage or lady garden prior to sex.*

Drag queen/king: *A performer who wears clothes traditionally assigned to the opposite gender.*

Fellatio: *Fancy term for oral sex on a dude.*

Foreskin: *Loose skin at the end of the penis.*

Gay: *Term to describe a homosexual man or woman.*

Glory hole: *A hole in a wall or partition through which a man pokes his peenie.*

Grindr: *A social network app for gay and bi men.*

HIV: *A virus affecting the immune system.*

Intersectionality: *The different parts of your whole identity and the impact they have on your life.*

Intersex: *Term to describe a person born with no clear gender or attributes of both genders.*

Labia: *The folds at the entrance of the vagina.*

Lesbian: *A homosexual woman.*

Lube: *Short for lubricant. Makes sex easier.*

Orgasm: *Sexual climax.*

Orgy: *Group sex.*

Penis: *Male erogenous zone.*

Poppers: *Slang term for amyl nitrite – an aroma that gives a feeling of light-headedness.*

Queer/genderqueer: *A person who refuses to label their sexuality or gender.*

Rimming: *Licking the bot-bot.*

Scat: *Eating poop.*

Scissor sisters: *A sexual position for two women OR an early 2000s electropop band.*

Strap-on: *A sex toy worn on a belt.*

STI: *Sexually transmitted infection.*

Sub: *Being the submissive partner during sex.*

Top/active: *Being the partner who 'gives' during sex.*

Transsexual: *Any person changing their gender identity.*

Transvestite: *A person who wears the clothes traditionally assigned to the opposite gender.*

Vibrator: *A vibrating sex toy.*

Water sports / golden shower: *Weeing on people in a way considered sexy.*

Helpful Numbers and Websites and Stuff

You are not alone. The Internet is jam-packed with services especially for young LGBT* people. The aim is to provide you with information, friends, contacts and condoms. Obviously, Google is your best friend, but here are some links and numbers to save you some time.

NHS Services

The NHS Live Well service has information on gay health, including HIV/AIDS: www.nhs.uk/Livewell/LGBhealth

The NHS also has fantastic advice for people thinking about their gender identity or transitioning. This site offers information and will also direct you to your nearest gender clinic: www.nhs.uk/Livewell/Transhealth

For information on STIs or to locate your nearest sexual health clinic: www.nhs.uk/Livewell/STIs

Helplines

The London Lesbian and Gay Switchboard offers advice to all LGBT* people on coming out, family, isolation, sex and sexual health, and even your nearest gay services, organisations, bars, and clubs. The calls are charged at the local rate and are included in your free mobile minutes.

LLGS: **0300 330 0630**

LGBT Helpline Scotland: **0300 123 2523**

Childline is free and confidential, 24 hours a day, 7 days a week, 365 days a year.

ChildLine: **0800 1111**

Charities and Pressure Groups

Stonewall: stonewall.org.uk

The Terrance Higgins Trust (for information on HIV/AIDS): tht.org.uk

The Kaleidoscope Trust: kaleidoscopetrust.com

Amnesty International: amnesty.org.uk

Mermaids Family Support Group for Children and Teenagers with Gender Identity Issues: mermaidsuk.org.uk

LGBT* Youth Groups

Southern England

Mosaic LGBT Youth Centre (North and West London): mosaicyouth.org.uk

The Gap Youth Club (South London): ww3.wandsworth.gov.uk/csweb/cs/Gap-Youth-Club.aspx

Allsorts Youth Project (Brighton / South Coast):
www.allsortsyouth.org.uk

YAY! (You And Yourself! Cornwall):
www.lgbtqyouthcornwall.co.uk

Space Youth Project (Dorset): spaceyouthproject.co.uk

Midlands

Out Central (Birmingham): **0121 464 5559**

Outburst (Nottingham): www.outburst.org.uk

North of England and Scotland

LGYM (Lesbian and Gay Youth Manchester):
www.lgbtyouthnorthwest.org.uk

LGBT Youth York:
www.lgbyouthyork.org.uk

LGBT Youth Scotland:
www.lgbtyouth.org.uk

GYRO (Gay Youth R Out Liverpool):
www.ypas.org.uk

POUT (Lancashire): **0800 783 1524**

Out 2 25 (Leeds): **07903 319435.**

BLAGY (Bradford): **01274 395815.**

Ireland

Belong To will direct you to your nearest group: www.belongto.org

UK Gay Youth website for LGBT* people 25 and under, with links to many groups: www.gayyouthuk.org.uk/

The Terrence Higgins Trust runs a website especially for young gay men, with links to many more groups: www.ygm.org.uk

DISCRIMINATION AND BULLYING

In the workplace: Contact ACAS (Advisory, Conciliation and Arbitration Service) at acas.org.uk.

THIS IS BY NO MEANS A COMPLETE LIST. NEW GROUPS ARE STARTING ALL THE TIME, AND IT'S LIKELY THERE'S A YOUTH GROUP VERY CLOSE TO WHERE YOU LIVE.

WRITING THIS HERE BOOK

The *This Book Is Gay* survey was carried out in spring/summer 2013. From the three hundred respondents, case studies were chosen and interviewed more thoroughly. Some names have been changed to protect the confidentiality of some interviewees. A huge thank you to all who took part.

ACKNOWLEDGMENTS

So many people to thank on this one. Firstly a big
thank you to *everyone* who contributed both their time
and their stories to this book. I simply wouldn't have
done it without you, seriously. Special thanks to All
Sorts Youth Group in Brighton and Wayne Dhesi at
Stonewall.

Thanks again to Tori Kosara, my editor, who suggested
the project in the first place and also supported it
throughout. I wasn't sure there was a book here, but it
turns out there is, and it's one I think we can both be
proud of. The fantastic illustrations are once again
down to Spike Gerrell and I think you've brought the
words to life.

Thanks to everyone at Hot Key and Red Lemon. Non-
fiction is such a team effort. Thanks to Jet and Dan
for the cover and design and to Emma for overseeing
everything. SPAM team: love you long time.

Finally, thanks as ever to Jo, my fantastic agent!

Queen of Teen 2014 Juno Dawson is the multi award-winning author of dark teen thrillers *Hollow Pike*, *Cruel Summer*, *Say Her Name* and *Under My Skin*, written under the name James Dawson. In 2015, she released her first contemporary romance, *All of the Above*. Her first non-fiction book, *Being a Boy*, tackled puberty, sex and relationships.

Juno is a regular contributor to *Attitude*, *GT*, *Glamour* and the *Guardian* and has contributed to news items concerning sexuality, identity, literature and education on *BBC Woman's Hour*, *Front Row*, *This Morning* and *Newsnight*. She is a School Role Model for the charity Stonewall, and also works with charity First Story to visit schools serving low income communities. Juno's titles have received rave reviews and her books have been translated into more than ten languages.

In 2015, Juno announced her transition to become a woman, having lived thus far as the male author James Dawson. She writes full time and lives in Brighton. Follow Juno on Twitter: @junodawson or on Facebook at Juno Dawson Books.